Iron Deficiency Anemia Cookbook US 2022

The Ultimate Anemia Guide with Over 100 Proven, Iron Rich, Easy and Delicious Recipes for a Sustainable Healthy Life. 28 Day Meal Plan and Journal Included.

Emma Jones

Table of Contents

Introduction

Iron deficiency anemia is a pretty common condition. You probably have heard someone talk about feeling low on iron. You might have even self-diagnosed iron deficiency just because you're feeling weak or experiencing a consistent loss of appetite.

You may not know that iron deficiency is a serious condition that affects many people. It is the most common type of anemia which is a blood disorder. It means a strict diet and iron supplements for people with severe conditions.

What is iron-deficiency anemia? How do you know if you have the deficiency? What causes this anemia, and how can you treat it? We have explained everything you might want to know about this common anemia.

Everything to Know About Iron Deficiency Anemia

Iron deficiency anemia is a red blood cell disorder caused by a lack of iron. Insufficient iron in the body makes it hard for the body to produce hemoglobin. Hemoglobin is a protein that helps your red blood cells to carry oxygen.

That's why this deficiency causes shortness of breath and tiredness. Your blood doesn't have the oxygen that your tissues and organs need. Since your body needs oxygen to function properly, it begins to shut down and can lead to serious issues.

However, many people suffer from mild iron deficiency for years without even knowing it. For severe cases of iron deficiency, the symptoms are harder to ignore. Regardless of how you are feeling, don't self-diagnose your iron deficiency.

If you suspect you have this anemia, talk to your doctor. But, how do you know that iron deficiency might be a possibility? Let's look at the types, causes, and symptoms of iron deficiency that will help you know whether you stand the risk.

Types, Causes, and Symptoms of Iron Deficiency Anemia

Anemia affects more than 30% of the world's population. According to WHO, 42% of children below 5 and 40% of pregnant women globally are anemic. More than two billion people globally and over three million Americans have anemia.

An anemic person does not have enough red blood cells in their body. While the drop in red blood cells could result from different reasons, iron deficiency anemia is the most common type of anemia. However, there are other types.

Other Types of Anemia

Iron deficiency anemia might be the only type of anemia that you know. But, other types can be inherited or acquired. Let's examine some of these other types of anemia.

- **Hemolytic Anemia**

This anemia results from acquired or inherited diseases. The diseases cause deformed red blood cells, making them easily destroyed in tight spaces such as capillaries, reducing their life span. Sickle cell anemia is one of the genetic forms of this condition.

- **Sickle Cell Anemia**

Individuals with this genetic anemia have abnormal sickle-shaped red blood cells with hemoglobin S. Red blood cells should normally be bi-concave. The sickle-shaped cells cause low oxygen tension in the tissues, making the individual feel pain.

- **Aplastic Anemia**

This anemia results from a malfunction of bone marrows, causing inadequate production of red blood cells. This condition can be congenital (from birth) or acquired (radiation and other chemicals like insecticides). It is also called bone marrow aplasia (failure).

- **Megaloblastic Anemia**

This anemia is caused by folic acid, intrinsic factor, and vitamin B12 deficiency leading to the slow development of erythroblasts in the bone marrow. These red blood cells are called "megaloblasts" as they are large with odd shapes.

- **Pernicious Anemia**

Pernicious anemia is strictly caused by a lack of intrinsic factor which allows for the absorption of vitamin B12. The lack of vitamin B12 makes it impossible to develop healthy red blood cells.

You might have noted that these types of anemia are either inherited or acquired. They are all also caused by one factor or the other. But, iron deficiency anemia is our focus. So, let's look into the possible causes of this anemia.

Anemia is not uncommon around the population. According to WHO, in between 1993 and 2005 approximately 1.6 billion people, which is 25% of the people globally, are anemic. Here are a variety of anemia.

A chronic consumption of alcohol consistently leads to lower folate levels. While the main problem with alcoholism is nutritional deficiency, it may cause anemia due to it affecting the bone marrow directly.

Other Types

There are various other types of anemia, most of which are uncommon. But it's important to be aware of them. These types are as follows:

- **Hemolytic Anemia**

This type of anemia is characterized when the body destroys red blood cells earlier than it should. Hemolytic anemia could result from an excessive amount of RBCs and it can also be the result of the genetic make of the body, and the body attacking itself.

- **Sickle Cell Anemia**

In this type of anemia, red blood cells are sickle-shaped and these cells break down rapidly. Red blood cells should normally be in a convex shape so that they have low oxygen levels of RBCs, so it will affect the individual not quite.

- **Aplastic Anemia**

Aplastic anemia is a rare type of anemia occurring when the body does not make enough RBCs. This condition results in pregnancy, chemotherapy, radiation, and other medications. It might result once someone has another disease.

- **Megaloblastic Anemia**

This anemia is caused by both folate deficiency and also by medication. It is the slow development of an individual's cells. It is the formation. These red blood cells are called megaloblasts, as they are larger and abnormal.

- **Pernicious Anemia**

Pernicious anemia is a type of anemia that occurs once someone has low absorption of Vitamin B12. This is why anemia that this kind may be due to the blood cells.

What may happen is that these types of anemia are either undiagnosed or the result of the combination of the types. Some individuals might suffer from it as little as possible.

Causes of Iron Deficiency Anemia

Iron deficiency is caused by a lack of iron in the body, but there are different underlying reasons why you might have a deficient iron level. Some of the reasons why you might have low iron levels include:

- **Inadequate Diet**

If you are not eating enough meals with iron, it can result in iron deficiency anemia. Foods like meat, eggs, and green vegetables are rich in the iron content that your body needs.

The exclusion of most of these foods in a vegetarian's diet is why they suffer from iron deficiency more than others. However, there are vegetables that a vegetarian can take to maintain the iron balance.

Don't go on a diet without ensuring all the nutrients your body needs are provided. As a man between 19 and 50, you need at least 8 milligrams of iron daily. Women from 50 years and younger need at least 18 milligrams daily. Pregnant women need as much as 27 milligrams of iron. You can consult a nutritionist if you're not sure your diet has adequate iron.

- **Internal Blood Loss**

Some medical conditions cause internal bleeding and this loss of blood results in a drop in iron levels. These conditions include colon cancer, stomach ulcer, hernia, colon polyps, and uterine fibroids. Regular use of some pain relievers like aspirin can cause stomach bleeding, which leads to iron deficiency.

- **Pregnancy**

Pregnant women need more oxygen for the baby. There is also an increased blood volume which demands more iron. If the pregnant woman's diet is not adjusted accordingly, it can lead to iron-deficiency anemia.

- **Heavy Menstruation**

People with heavy menstruation often lose a lot of blood, resulting in iron deficiency. The blood loss could also be a result of endometriosis. Many people don't know that they even have it. You can resolve this iron deficiency by treating the underlying causes using birth control pills or devices.

- **Slow Absorption of Iron**

Due to conditions like celiac disease, Crohn's disease, or ulcerative colitis, your body might find it hard to absorb iron from your small intestine meals. In this case, it is not a matter of taking enough iron but the inability of your body to absorb it. Surgeries like a gastric bypass can also demand the removal of parts of the intestine, making it harder for your body to absorb iron.

Genetic conditions and injuries which cause a lot of blood loss can also lead to iron deficiency in the body. If you have any of these causes, you might want to check for symptoms of iron deficiency.

Who is at Risk?

From the causes, it is clear that women are more likely to suffer from this deficiency. They have a higher need for iron daily and even more when pregnant or menstruating.

This figure doesn't mean that men and children don't get iron deficient. People at risk of having iron deficiency include:

- Premature or low weight babies
- Children going through a growth spurt
- Blood donors
- People with a family history of anemia
- Women with reproductive years
- People with intestinal disorders and chronic illnesses
- Vegetarians

You belong to a group of people at risk of iron deficiency doesn't mean you have the condition. If you think you are low on iron, you can watch out for symptoms.

Symptoms of Iron Deficiency

Generally, people that are anemic have similar symptoms. Therefore, it is essential that you go to a doctor to diagnose whether you have iron-deficiency anemia. The symptoms can be pointed toward something more serious or even inaccurate. So, see a doctor before taking any steps.

- Headaches
- Dizziness
- Extreme fatigue
- General weakness
- Shortness of breath
- Faster Heartbeat
- Pale skin
- Brittle nails
- Chest pain
- Cold hands and feet
- Tingling feeling in legs
- Tongue inflammation or soreness
- Poor appetite
- Pica (an unusual craving for non-nutritive things like ice or dirt)

Weight loss is also a possible when you have iron-deficiency anemia. Studies have shown that people who are overweight lose weight when they have low iron. It could also occur in people that have other underlying causes like cancer. You might also get anemic if you had a weight loss surgery due to vitamin and mineral deficiencies.

If you exhibit some of these symptoms, a simple routine blood test can tell you if you have iron deficiency. However, do not resort to taking iron supplements without a doctor's recommendation. Excess iron in your blood can cause other health conditions like liver damage and constipation. In young children, it can be fatal.

How to Diagnose Iron Deficiency

Only a medical professional can diagnose you with iron deficiency anemia. Once you notice any of these symptoms, see your doctor. Don't just assume you know what it is and start changing your diet or taking supplements.

It takes a medical examination to know if you have iron deficiency. During the exam, the doctor would ask questions about your general health. Your fingernails, skin tone, and under your eyelids might be examined for physical signs of the condition.

But, visible signs do not give a conclusive diagnosis for this condition. The symptoms are similar to other conditions, so a blood test would be taken to remove all doubts. Your doctor will examine your blood for the red blood cell count, size and color of the RBC, low ferritin levels, and hemoglobin levels.

Low red blood cell count, abnormal size of the color of the cells, low ferritin levels, and low hemoglobin levels are indicators of anemia. Your doctor might have to do a further examination to determine the cause of the anemia and prescribe the right treatment.

The additional tests could be an endoscopy, a colonoscopy, or a fecal occult test, depending on what your doctor perceives to be the cause. An endoscopy examines your esophagus and upper small intestine lining.

A colonoscopy examines your colon lining. A fecal occult test examines for blood in your feces. Based on the test results, your doctor will know the next step. In the case of internal bleeding, the next step is to stop the bleeding, which might require surgery.

Whatever the doctor's diagnosis might be as to the cause, you want to start consciously managing the condition with the right meals. There are foods that you can take to help you improve the iron levels in your bloodstream.

Foods to Treat Anemia

Once you have been diagnosed with anemia, the doctor will try to find the condition's root cause. If it is a lack of iron, you might be given iron supplements to boost the iron levels in your body.

You might also be given vitamin C supplements to aid iron absorption. Most people take about 150 to 200 milligrams of iron supplements daily. But, you should always take the dosage recommended by your doctor based on your iron levels. Iron supplements might have their side effects: nausea, vomiting, black poo, diarrhea, heartburn, and tummy pain. But you should not stop taking the supplements because of these side effects. Your doctor will tell you when to stop after conducting a test to know whether your iron levels have been restored to normal. If you suffer from low iron absorption, your doctor might have to do a transfusion of red blood cells into your body. This transfusion will help to boost your iron levels before the underlying cause is treated.

However, you can change your diet to combat this deficiency faster. If you eat certain foods and avoid some, you will naturally boost your iron levels. Paying close attention to your diet can help you treat anemia without any side effects.

Foods to Avoid to Treat Anemia

Certain foods can impede the absorption of iron in your body. While you take iron supplements, it is important to avoid these foods as much as possible. Note that you don't have to eliminate any food from your diet, but you can reduce your intake.

Some of the foods to avoid or reduce include:

- Foods with tannin like tea, coffee, and some spices
- Soy protein
- Too much fiber
- Milk
- Wine and beer

While you try to reduce the intake of some foods to allow your body to absolve iron, you also need to take iron-rich foods and foods that aid iron absorption. You should also not take calcium with your iron supplements.

You might also want to eliminate junks from the menu as they don't do your body any good. It only adds to your calories without any nutrients. The right meals will, however, lead you to sound health.

Foods to Eat to Treat Anemia

Eating well to treat anemia is possible. You just have to know which foods to eat. While some foods will increase your iron levels, others will make it easier for your body to absorb the dietary iron. It is essential that you take these foods together. You can have balanced delicious meals that combine all these foods. For instance, you can take orange juice with your iron supplements (orange has vitamin C that aids the absorption of iron).

Some iron-rich foods to add to your diet include:

- Meat like chicken, beef, turkey, lamb, liver, and pork
- Beans
- Pumpkin and squash seeds
- Peas, black-eyed peas, and lima beans
- Leafy greens like spinach, kale, turnip greens, and collard greens
- Eggs
- Seafood like shrimps, sardines, oysters, and clams
- Dried fruits like raisins and prunes
- Iron-enriched cereals (dry or instant)

You can see that you have a wide array of foods to choose from in preparing meals that'll aid your iron deficiency treatment. You also need to ensure that you accompany these iron foods with foods that will aid the iron absorption in the meal.

Some foods that aid the absorption of iron in the body include:

- Citrus fruits like oranges
- Berries
- Whole grains
- Dark leafy vegetables
- Red and green bell peppers
- Brussel sprouts
- Tomatoes
- Cauliflower

These foods contain vitamins and nutrients that aid the digestion of iron. You will find your daily requirements of vitamin B and other vitamins met by eating these foods. You can consult a dietitian to help you structure your meals, especially if you have a severe case of iron deficiency. You can prepare more meals with these foods for a mild case, and your iron levels will gradually rise.

Tips and Tricks to Achieve the Perfect Iron Balance

Before we get into the tips and tricks, the first thing you should know is that there is no magic to having a perfect iron balance. Even with these tips and tricks, it will take consistency and commitment to your health to maintain your iron balance.

- **Eat Meat**

There are two sources of iron; heme iron from animal-based foods and non-heme iron from plant-based foods. Heme iron from animal-based foods is easily absorbed into the bloodstream compared to non-heme iron.

So, eating meat such as red meat can drastically change the iron levels in your body. You can still get your iron from plant-based foods like tofu, spinach, and legumes for vegetarians.

However, note that only about two to twenty percent of the iron in plant-based foods makes its way into the bloodstream from your digestive tract. Animal-based foods like meat yield up to fifteen to thirty-five percent of the iron into the bloodstream. If you can, eat meat and cut the process.

- **Take Vitamin C**

Vitamin C speeds up the absorption of iron in your body. As a vegetarian, you can mix your meals with vitamin C-rich fruits and vegetables like oranges, kiwis, grapefruits, and bell peppers.

You don't have to be a vegetarian to eat these fruits and vegetables. Add them to your meals daily, and you can make the most of your iron-rich foods.

- **Cook with Cast-Iron Skillet**

Cooking with iron cookware can increase the iron content in your food, especially for acidic foods with high moisture. Foods like tomato sauce cooked in iron cookware have higher iron content.

Studies show that cooking with a cast iron pot increases iron content by 16%. So, note that your cooking can help you get more iron in your meals.

- **Reschedule the Tannin**

As we have explained before, coffee and tea contain tannin, making iron hard to absorb. So, while you can still take your coffee and tea, you should not take them with your iron-rich meals. Plan your meals and take the beverages a few hours before or after your iron-rich meals.

- **Space out the Iron**

You might feel tempted to eat all the iron in one meal. But, this strategy doesn't work. It is best to eat different iron foods in your meals in small doses. Infusing iron-rich ingredients in your meals works better than eating all the iron in one meal.

Iron deficiency anemia can be treated. You just need to pay attention to your meals and use your medications as prescribed by your doctor.

What Happens if You Don't Treat Iron Deficiency Anemia

While most types of anemia can be treated, people can still die from anemia. According to the Center for Disease Control and Prevention, 1.7 people in every 100,000 died of anemia in 2017.

Many people suffer from iron deficiency anemia, and it often goes untreated in some people. However, the consequences of leaving iron deficiency untreated can be fatal. Some of the complications that can arise from untreated iron-deficiency anemia include:

- Depression
- Preterm delivery and low weight babies for pregnant women
- Higher risk of infection due to a defective immune system
- Slow developmental growth in children which can include motor and cognitive problems
- Heart problems that can lead up to a heart failure

Iron deficiency anemia can kill you, whether you know you have it or don't. Even if you are in the at-risk groups, you might want to ensure you carry out a routine blood test and take the necessary steps to prevent this anemia.

If not, you still want to stay healthy, and eating iron-rich meals can help you maintain a perfect iron balance. Whether at risk or not, everyone needs to eat the right amount of iron in their meals.

That's what this cookbook is all about – helping you maintain a perfect iron balance in your meals. You will find the meals in this book delicious and iron-rich. So, get ready to give your red blood cells a feast!

Breakfast Recipes

Greens & Fruit Smoothie

Servings|2   Time|10 minutes
Nutritional Content (per serving):
Cal| 113   Fat| 0.5g   Protein| 3.8g   Carbs| 25.7g   Fiber| 3g

Ingredients:

- Fresh pineapple (1 cup)
- Fresh kale (2 cups)
- Fresh lemon juice (2 tablespoons)
- Fresh baby spinach (2 cups)
- Fresh orange juice (½ cup)
- Chilled water (12 ounces)

Directions:

1. In a high-power blender, add all ingredients and pulse until smooth.
2. Transfer the smoothie into two serving glasses and serve immediately.

Green Tofu Smoothie

Servings|2   Time|10 minutes
Nutritional Content (per serving):
Cal| 114   Fat| 5.2g   Protein| 7.8g   Carbs| 10.8g   Fiber| 2.2g

Ingredients:

- Fresh spinach (2 cups)
- Silken tofu (6 ounces)
- Ice cubes (¼ cup)
- Frozen mango chunks (½ cup)
- Unsweetened almond milk (1½ cups)

Directions:

1. In a high-power blender, add all ingredients and pulse until smooth.

2. Transfer the smoothie into two serving glasses and serve immediately.

Spinach & Strawberry Smoothie

Servings|2 Time|10 minutes
Nutritional Content (per serving):
Cal| 86   Fat| 0.6g   Protein| 2.2g   Carbs| 19.5g   Fiber| 2.4g

Ingredients:

- ❖ Frozen strawberries (1 cup)
- ❖ Fresh orange juice (1 cup)
- ❖ Fresh spinach (2 cups)
- ❖ Chilled water (1 cup)

Directions:

1. In a high-power blender, add all ingredients and pulse until smooth.
2. Transfer the smoothie into two serving glasses and serve immediately.

Spinach & Avocado Smoothie

Servings|2 Time|10 minutes
Nutritional Content (per serving):
Cal| 132   Fat| 11.7g   Protein| 3.1g   Carbs| 6.1g   Fiber| 4.5g

Ingredients:

- ❖ Fresh baby spinach (2 cups)
- ❖ Liquid stevia (4-6 drops)
- ❖ Hemp seeds (1 tablespoon)
- ❖ Avocado (½, peeled, pitted and chopped)
- ❖ Chilled water (2 cups)

Directions:

1. In a high-power blender, add all ingredients and pulse until smooth.

2. Transfer the smoothie into two serving glasses and serve immediately.

Apple Oat Smoothie

Servings|2   Time|10 minutes
Nutritional Content (per serving):
Cal| 178   Fat| 3.7g   Protein| 3g   Carbs| 37.1g   Fiber| 6g

Ingredients:

- Large apple (1, peeled, core and sliced)
- Old-fashioned oats (¼ cup)
- Ice cubes (¼ cup)
- Large banana (1, peeled and sliced)
- Unsweetened almond milk (1½ cups)

Directions:

1. In a high-power blender, add all ingredients and pulse until smooth.
2. Transfer the smoothie into two serving glasses and serve immediately.

Spinach Smoothie Bowl

Servings|2   Time|10 minutes
Nutritional Content (per serving):
Cal| 386   Fat| 25.2g   Protein| 17.5g   Carbs| 27.1g   Fiber| 9.1g

Ingredients:

- Fresh spinach (2 cups)
- Unsweetened protein powder (1 scoop)
- Fresh lemon juice (2 tablespoons)
- Ice cubes (¼ cup)
- Fresh strawberries (¼ cup, hulled and sliced)
- Medium avocado (1, peeled, pitted and chopped roughly)
- Maple syrup (2 tablespoons)
- Unsweetened almond milk (1 cup)
- Almonds (2 tablespoons, chopped)

Directions:

1. In a high-powder blender, add all the ingredients except for almonds and strawberries and pulse until smooth.
2. Transfer into 2 serving bowls and serve with the topping of almonds and strawberries.

Simple Oatmeal

Servings|2   Time|10 minutes
Nutritional Content (per serving):
Cal| 207   Fat| 6.2g   Protein| 5.3g   Carbs| 35g   Fiber| 3.8g

Ingredients:

- Steel-cut oats (½ cup)
- Maple syrup (2 tablespoons)
- Walnuts (2 tablespoons)
- Water (2 cups)
- Large peach (1, pitted and chopped)

Directions:

1. In a small-sized saucepan, add water and oats over medium-high heat and bring to a boil.
2. Now adjust the heat to low and simmer for about 20 minutes, stirring occasionally.
3. Remove from heat and stir in the maple syrup.
4. Serve warm with the topping of peach slices and almonds.

Blueberry Oatmeal

Servings|2   Time|20 minutes
Nutritional Content (per serving):
Cal| 341   Fat| 7.9g   Protein| 10.9g   Carbs| 59.4g   Fiber| 7.1g

Ingredients:

- Unsweetened soy milk (2 cups)
- Frozen blueberries (½ cup)
- Fresh lemon juice (1 tablespoon)
- Almonds (2 tablespoons, chopped)
- Oats (1 cup)
- Maple syrup (2 tablespoons)
- Small banana (1, peeled and sliced)

Directions:

1. In a saucepan, add the soy milk, oats and blueberries over medium heat and cook for about 8-10 minutes or until desired thickness of oatmeal.
2. Remove from the heat and stir in the maple syrup and lemon juice.
3. Serve with the topping of banana slices and almonds.

Nuts & Seeds Porridge

Servings|4   Time|45 minutes
Nutritional Content (per serving):
Cal| 227   Fat| 21g   Protein| 5.8g   Carbs| 8.9g   Fiber| 6.2g

Ingredients:

- Pecans (1/3 cup)
- Sunflower seeds (¼ cup)
- Unsweetened coconut flakes (¼ cup)
- Water (2½-3 cups)

- Almonds (1/3 cup)
- Chia seeds (¼ cup)
- Unsweetened almond milk (1 cup)

Directions:

1. In a food processor, place the pecans, walnuts and sunflower seeds and pulse until a crumbly mixture is formed.
2. In a medium-sized saucepan, add the nuts mixture, chia seeds, coconut flakes, almond milk and water over medium heat and bring to a gentle simmer, stirring frequently.
3. Now adjust the heat to low and simmer for about 20-30 minutes, stirring frequently.
4. Serve hot.

Oats & Quinoa Porridge

Servings|3   Time|35 minutes
Nutritional Content (per serving):
Cal| 304   Fat| 9.6g   Protein| 8.9g   Carbs| 48g   Fiber| 7.1g

Ingredients:

- Unsweetened almond milk (2 cups)
- Dried quinoa (¼ cup, rinsed)
- Chia seeds (1 tablespoon)
- Vanilla extract (½ teaspoon)
- Fresh strawberries (¼ cup, hulled and sliced)
- Water (2 cups)
- Old-fashioned oats (1 cup)
- Flaxseeds (1 tablespoon)
- Maple syrup (3 tablespoons)
- Almonds (3 tablespoons, chopped)
- Fresh blueberries (¼ cup)

Directions:

1. In a saucepan, mix together all the ingredients except the pumpkin seeds and berries over medium heat and bring to a gentle boil.
2. Cook for about 20 minutes, stirring occasionally.
3. Stir in chopped dates and immediately remove from heat.
4. Serve warm with the garnishing of berries and almonds.

Tofu & Spinach Scramble

Servings|2   Time|23 minutes
Nutritional Content (per serving):
Cal| 134   Fat| 10.1g   Protein| 8.5g   Carbs| 5.8g   Fiber| 2.7g

Ingredients:

- Olive oil (1 tablespoon)
- Medium-firm tofu ((¼ pound), drained, pressed and crumbled)
- Low-sodium soy sauce (2 teaspoons)
- Garlic clove (1, minced)
- Vegetable broth (1/3 cup)
- Fresh baby spinach (2¾ cups)
- Ground turmeric (1 teaspoon)
- Fresh lemon juice (1 teaspoon)

Directions:

1. Heat olive oil in a frying saucepan over medium-high heat and sauté the garlic for about 1 minute.
2. Add the tofu and cook for about 2-3 minutes, slowly adding the broth.
3. Add the spinach, soy sauce and turmeric and stir fry for about 3-4 minutes or until all the liquid is absorbed.
4. Stir in the lemon juice and serve immediately.

Spicy Tofu & Veggie Scramble

Servings|2   Time|31 minutes
Nutritional Content (per serving):
Cal| 278   Fat| 20.9g   Protein| 13.9g   Carbs| 13.9g   Fiber| 2.4g

Ingredients:

For Sauce:

- Garlic powder (½ teaspoon)
- Ground cumin (½ teaspoon)
- Ground turmeric (¼ teaspoon)
- Red chili powder (¼ teaspoon)
- Paprika (1/8 teaspoon)
- Salt and ground black pepper, as required
- Water, as required

For Scramble:

- Olive oil (2 tablespoons)
- Bell pepper (½, seeded and chopped)
- Red onion (¼, chopped)
- Fresh baby spinach (2 cups)
- Extra-firm tofu (8 ounces, pressed, drained and pat dried)

Directions:

1. For sauce: in a bowl, add all the spices and enough water and cook until a slightly thin sauce is formed.
2. In a large wok, heat the oil over medium heat and cook the bell pepper, onion, salt and black pepper for about 5 minutes, stirring frequently.
3. Stir in the kale and cook, covered for about 2 minutes.
4. Meanwhile, in a bowl, place the tofu and with a fork, crumble into bite-sized pieces.
5. With a spatula, move the veggies to one side of the wok.
6. Add the tofu and sauté for about 2 minutes.
7. Add the sauce and immediately stir the mixture well.
8. Cook for another 5-7 minutes or until tofu is slightly browned, stirring frequently.
9. Serve hot.

Black Beans & Egg Scramble

Servings|2 Time|25 minutes
Nutritional Content (per serving):
Cal| 167   Fat| 9.6g   Protein| 9.3g   Carbs| 11.8g   Fiber| 2.9g

Ingredients:

- Olive oil (3 teaspoons)
- Shallot (1, sliced thinly)
- Eggs (2, lightly beaten)
- Fresh parsley (1 tablespoon, chopped)
- Canned black beans (5½ ounces, rinsed and drained)
- Salt and ground black pepper, as required

Directions:

1. In a non-stick wok, heat the oil over low heat and cook the beans and shallot for about 10 minutes, stirring occasionally.
2. Add the eggs and black pepper and cook for about 3-5 minutes or until done completely, stirring continuously.
3. Serve immediately with the garnishing of parsley.

Eggless Spinach Omelet

Servings|2   Time|25 minutes
Nutritional Content (per serving):
Cal| 270   Fat| 16.2g   Protein| 2.4g   Carbs| 23g   Fiber| 4.9g

Ingredients:

- Chickpeas flour (¾ cup)
- Salt and ground black pepper, as required
- Tomato (½ cup, seeded and chopped finely)
- Vegetable oil (2 tablespoons)
- Cumin seeds (½ teaspoon)
- Water (½ cup)
- Fresh spinach (1½ cups, chopped finely)
- Green chili (1, chopped finely)

Directions:

1. In a bowl, add the chickpeas flour, cumin seeds, salt and black pepper and mix well.
2. Slowly, add the water slowly and mix until a smooth mixture is formed.
3. Add the vegetables and green chili and stir to combine.
4. In a non-stick wok, heat 1 tablespoon of the oil over medium heat.
5. Add about ½ C. of the mixture into the wok and with the back of a spoon, spread into a 7-inch circle.
6. Spread about 2 teaspoons of oil over the veggie mixture and cook for about 30 seconds.
7. Flip the omelet and cook or about 2-3 minutes, flipping and pressing the omelet 2-3 times.
8. Repeat with the remaining veggie mixture.
9. Serve hot.

Greens Quiche

Servings|4   Time|35 minutes
Nutritional Content (per serving):
Cal| 176   Fat| 10.9g   Protein| 15.4g   Carbs| 5g   Fiber| 0.9g

Ingredients:

- ❖ Eggs (6)
- ❖ Salt and ground black pepper, as required
- ❖ Fresh baby kale (1 cup, chopped)
- ❖ Scallion (1, chopped)
- ❖ Fresh cilantro (¼ cup, chopped)
- ❖ Mozzarella cheese (3 tablespoons, grated)
- ❖ Unsweetened almond milk (½ cup)
- ❖ Fresh baby spinach (1 cup, chopped)
- ❖ Green bell pepper (½ cup, seeded and chopped)
- ❖ Fresh chives (1 tablespoon, minced)

Directions:

1. Preheat your oven to 400 degrees F. Lightly grease a pie dish.
2. In a large bowl, add the eggs, almond milk, salt and black pepper and beat until well combined.
3. In another bowl, add the vegetables and herbs and mix well.
4. In the bottom of prepared pie dish, place the veggie mixture evenly and top with the egg mixture.
5. Bake for approximately 20 minutes or until a wooden skewer inserted in the center comes out clean.
6. Remove from the oven and immediately sprinkle with the Parmesan cheese.
7. Set aside for about 5 minutes before slicing.
8. Cut into desired-sized wedges and serve.

Eggs with Spinach

Servings|2   Time|32 minutes
Nutritional Content (per serving):
Cal| 172   Fat| 11.2g   Protein| 15g   Carbs| 4.4g   Fiber| 2g

Ingredients:

- ❖ Fresh baby spinach (6 cups)
- ❖ Feta cheese (3 tablespoons, crumbled)
- ❖ Fresh chives (3 teaspoon, minced)
- ❖ Water (2-3 tablespoons)
- ❖ Eggs (4)
- ❖ Ground black pepper, as required

Directions:

1. Preheat your oven to 400 degrees F. Lightly grease 2 small baking dishes.
2. In a large frying saucepan, add the spinach and water over medium heat and cook for about 3-4 minutes, stirring occasionally.
3. Remove from the heat and drain the excess water completely.
4. Divide the spinach into prepared baking dishes evenly.
5. Carefully crack 2 eggs in each baking dish over spinach.
6. Sprinkle with black pepper and top with feta cheese evenly.
7. Arrange the baking dishes onto a large cookie sheet.
8. Bake for approximately 15-18 minutes or until desired doneness of eggs.
9. Serve hot with the garnishing of chives.

Tempeh Hash

Servings|3   Time|45 minutes
Nutritional Content (per serving):
Cal| 250   Fat| 15.9g   Protein| 1.6g   Carbs| 26g   Fiber| 5g

Ingredients:

- Medium sweet potato (1, peeled and chopped)
- Garlic cloves (2, chopped finely)
- Fresh kale (3 cups, tough ribs removed and chopped)
- Nutritional yeast (2 tablespoons)
- Ground black pepper (¼ teaspoon)
- Extra-virgin olive oil (2 tablespoons, divided)
- Medium onion (½, chopped)
- Tempeh (½ cup, crumbled)
- Apple cider vinegar (2 tablespoons)
- Cayenne pepper (½ teaspoon)
- Paprika (½ teaspoon)

Directions:

1. Preheat your oven to 425 degrees F. Line a 10-inch×15-inch baking sheet with a piece of foil.
2. In a small bowl, place the sweet potato pieces and 1 tablespoon of oil and toss to coat well.
3. Place the sweet potato pieces onto the prepared baking sheet and spread in an even layer.
4. Bake for approximately 20 minutes.
5. In a large wok, heat the remaining oil over medium-low heat and sauté the garlic for about 1 minute.
6. Add the onion and sauté for about 3 minutes.
7. Add kale and sauté for about 2 minutes.
8. Add the tempeh and cook for about 1 minute, stirring frequently.
9. Stir in the sweet potatoes, vinegar, nutritional yeast paprika and cayenne pepper and cook for about 1-2 minutes, stirring continuously.
10. Stir in the black pepper and remove from the heat.
11. Serve warm.

Veggie Saucepancake

Servings|2   Time|27 minutes
Nutritional Content (per serving):
Cal| 224   Fat| 6.7g   Protein| 10.2g   Carbs| 33g   Fiber| 9.7g

Ingredients:

- Water (1 cup)
- Ground turmeric (1 teaspoon)
- Salt and ground black pepper, as required
- Spinach (¼ cup, chopped finely)
- Chickpea flour (1 cup)
- Red pepper flakes (½ teaspoon, crushed)
- Bell pepper (1, seeded and chopped finely)
- Olive oil (1 tablespoon)

Directions:

1. In a food processor, add the water, flour, turmeric, red pepper flakes, salt and black pepper and pulse until well combined.
2. Transfer the mixture into a bowl and set aside for about 3-5 minutes.
3. Add the bell pepper and spinach and mix well.
4. In a wok, heat the oil over medium heat.
5. Add half of the mixture and spread in an even layer.
6. Cook for about 5-6 minutes, flipping once after 3 minutes.
7. Repeat with the remaining mixture.
8. Serve warm.

Oatmeal Cottage Cheese Saucepancakes

Servings|4   Time|31 minutes
Nutritional Content (per serving):
Cal| 122   Fat| 3.7g   Protein| 10.3g   Carbs| 12.7g   Fiber| 2.4g

Ingredients:

- Cottage cheese (½ cup)
- Powdered peanuts (2 tablespoons)
- Instant oatmeal (½ cup)
- Large egg whites (4)
- Frozen mixed berries (1 cup)

Directions:

1. In a blender, add the cottage cheese, oatmeal, powdered peanuts and egg whites and pulse until smooth. (The mixture should be like a saucepancake batter).
2. Transfer the mixture into a mixing bowl.
3. Add the mixed berry blend and with a wooden spoon, gently stir to combine.
4. Heat a lightly greased non-stick wok over medium heat.
5. Add desired amount of the mixture and with a spoon, spread in an even layer.
6. Cook for about 2 minutes or until bottom becomes golden brown.
7. Carefully flip the side and cook for about 2 minutes more or until golden brown.
8. Repeat with the remaining mixture.
9. Serve warm.

Broccoli Muffins

Servings|6   Time|15 minutes
Nutritional Content (per serving):
Cal| 163   Fat| 14.2g   Protein| 7.3g   Carbs| 2.3g   Fiber| 0.6g

Ingredients:

- ❖ Coconut flour (1/3 cup)
- ❖ Salt and ground black pepper, as required
- ❖ Feta cheese (½ cup, crumbled)
- ❖ Parmesan cheese (¼ cup, grated)
- ❖ Baking powder (½ teaspoon)
- ❖ Eggs (4)
- ❖ Unsalted butter (¼ cup, melted)
- ❖ Cooked spinach (½ cup)
- ❖ Scallions (4, chopped)

Directions:

1. Preheat your oven to 4000 degrees F. Grease 12 cups of a muffin tin.
2. In a bowl, add the eggs, thyme, garlic powder, salt and black pepper and beat until well combined.
3. Add the broccoli and cheese and stir to combine.
4. Place the mixture into the prepared muffin cups about 2/3 full.
5. Bake for approximately 12-15 minutes or until tops become golden brown.
6. Remove the muffin tin from oven and place onto a wire rack to cool for about 10 minutes.
7. Carefully invert the muffins onto the wire rack and serve warm.

Tofu & Mushroom Muffins

Servings|6   Time|50 minutes
Nutritional Content (per serving):
Cal| 161   Fat| 3.1g   Protein| 5g   Carbs| 3.8g   Fiber| 0.5g

Ingredients:

- Olive oil (1 teaspoon)
- Scallion (1, chopped)
- Garlic (1 teaspoon, minced)
- Ground black pepper, as required
- Unsweetened almond milk (¼ cup)
- Arrowroot starch (1 tablespoon)
- Extra-virgin olive oil (¼ teaspoon)
- Fresh mushrooms (1½ cups, chopped)
- Fresh rosemary (1 teaspoon, minced)
- Silken tofu (1 (12.3-ounce) package, pressed and drained)
- Parmesan cheese (2 tablespoons, grated)
- Ground turmeric (¼ teaspoon)

Directions:

1. Preheat your oven to 375 degrees F. Grease 12 cups of a muffin tin.
2. In a non-stick wok, heat the oil over medium heat and sauté the scallion and garlic for about 1 minute.
3. Add the mushrooms and sauté for about 5-7 minutes.
4. Stir in the rosemary and black pepper and remove from the heat
5. Set aside to cool slightly.
6. In a food processor, add the tofu and remaining ingredients and pulse until smooth.
7. Transfer the tofu mixture into a large bowl.
8. Fold in the mushroom mixture.
9. Place the mixture into the prepared muffin cups evenly.
10. Bake for approximately 20-22 minutes or until a toothpick inserted in the center comes out clean.
11. Remove the muffin tin from the oven and place onto a wire rack to cool for about 10 minutes.
12. Carefully invert the muffins onto a platter and serve warm.

Tofu & Zucchini Muffins

Servings|6   Time|55 minutes
Nutritional Content (per serving):
Cal| 237   Fat| 9g   Protein| 11.1g   Carbs| 29.3g   Fiber| 5.9g

Ingredients:

- ❖ Extra-firm silken tofu (12 ounces, pressed and drained)
- ❖ Apple cider vinegar (1 tablespoon)
- ❖ Chickpea flour (½ cup)
- ❖ Baking soda (1 teaspoon)
- ❖ Onion powder (1 teaspoon)
- ❖ Zucchini (½ cup, chopped)
- ❖ Unsweetened soy milk (¾ cup)
- ❖ Canola oil (2 tablespoons)
- ❖ Whole-wheat pastry flour (1 cup)
- ❖ Baking powder (1 teaspoon)
- ❖ Smoked paprika (1 teaspoon)
- ❖ Salt (1 teaspoon)
- ❖ Fresh chives (¼ cup, minced)

Directions:

1. Preheat your oven to 400 degrees F. Line a 12 cups muffin tin with paper liners.
2. In a bowl, place tofu and with a fork, mash until smooth.
3. In the bowl of tofu, add almond milk, oil and vinegar and mix until slightly smooth.
4. In a separate large bowl, add flours, baking powder, baking soda spices and salt and mix well.
5. Transfer the mixture into prepared muffin cups evenly.
6. Bake for approximately 35-40 minutes or until a toothpick inserted in the center comes out clean.
7. Remove the muffin tin from oven and place onto a wire rack to cool for about 10 minutes.
8. Then invert the muffins onto a platter and serve warm.

Nuts & Seeds Bread

Servings|14   Time|1½ hours
Nutritional Content (per serving):
Cal| 174   Fat| 14g   Protein| 6g   Carbs| 10.1g   Fiber| 7.5g

Ingredients:

- Raw pumpkin seeds (½ cup)
- Raw almonds (½ cup)
- Chia seeds (½ cup)
- Psyllium husks (½ cup)
- Salt (1 teaspoon)
- Coconut oil (3 tablespoons, melted)
- Raw hazelnuts (½ cup)
- Raw sunflower seeds (1 cup)
- Golden flaxseeds (½ cup)
- Golden flaxseeds meal (¼ cup)
- Powdered stevia (1 teaspoon)
- Warm water (1½ cups)

Directions:

1. Preheat your oven to 350 degrees F. Line a bread loaf saucepan with parchment paper.
2. In a food processor, add the pumpkin seeds, hazelnuts and almonds and pulse until coarse flour-like mixture is formed.
3. Place nuts mixture, sunflower seeds, chia seeds, flaxseeds, psyllium husks, flaxseeds meal, salt, powder stevia, coconut oil and warm water in a large bowl and mix until well combined.
4. Place the mixture into the prepared bread loaf saucepan evenly and with your hands, press to smooth the top surface.
5. Bake for approximately 45 minutes.
6. With the help of the parchment paper, carefully transfer the bread loaf onto a baking sheet
7. Bake for approximately 15-25 minutes or until a wooden skewer inserted in the center comes out clean.
8. Remove the baking sheet from oven and place onto a wire rack to cool for about 15 minutes.
9. Now, invert the bread onto the wire rack to cool completely before slicing.
10. Cut the bread loaf into desired-sized slices and serve.

Raisin Bread

Servings|10   Time|45 minutes
Nutritional Content (per serving):
Cal| 164   Fat| 10.5g   Protein| 4.3g   Carbs| 15.3g   Fiber| 1.6g

Ingredients:

- Almond flour (2 cups)
- Baking soda (1 teaspoon)
- Salt (¼ teaspoon)
- Maple syrup (¼ cup)
- Vanilla extract (3 teaspoons)
- Ground cinnamon (2 tablespoons)
- Eggs (5)
- Coconut oil (¼ cup)
- Raisins (½ cup)

Directions:

1. Preheat your oven to 350 degrees F. Line a bread loaf saucepan with parchment paper.
2. Place almond flour, baking soda, cinnamon and salt in a bowl and mix well.
3. In another bowl, place eggs, maple syrup, coconut oil and vanilla extract and with an electric mixer, beat until well combined.
4. In the bowl of egg mixture, add flour mixture and mix until well combined.
5. Gently fold in the raisins.
6. Place the mixture into the prepared bread loaf saucepan evenly and with your hands, press to smooth the top surface.
7. Bake for approximately 30 minutes or until a wooden skewer inserted in the center comes out clean.
8. Remove the bread saucepan from oven and place onto a wire rack to cool for about 15 minutes.
9. Now, invert the bread onto the wire rack to cool completely before slicing.
10. With a sharp knife, cut the bread loaf into desired-sized slices and serve.

Dried Fruit Bread

Servings|10   Time|1 hour 10 minutes
Nutritional Content (per serving):
Cal| 140   Fat| 9.1g   Protein| 4.2g   Carbs| 11.4g   Fiber| 1g

Ingredients:

- Arrowroot powder (¼ cup)
- Salt (¼ teaspoon)
- Creamy almond butter (¾ cup, softened)
- Vanilla extract (1 teaspoon)
- Sunflower seeds (1/3 cup)
- Dried apricots (¼ cup, chopped finely)
- Baking soda (¼ teaspoon)
- Large eggs (3)
- Olive oil (2 tablespoons)
- Maple syrup (3 tablespoons)
- Pumpkin seeds (1/3 cup)
- Dried cranberries (½ cup)
- Almonds (¼ cup, chopped)

Directions:

1. Preheat your oven to 350 degrees F. Line a bread loaf saucepan with a lightly greased parchment paper.
2. Place arrowroot powder, baking soda, and salt in a large bowl and mix well.
3. In a separate bowl, add eggs, butter, oil, maple syrup and vanilla extract and beat until well combined.
4. Add egg mixture into bowl with flour mixture and mix until well combined.
5. Gently fold in seeds, dried fruit and almonds.
6. Place the bread mixture into the prepared loaf saucepan evenly.
7. Bake for approximately 40-50 minutes or until a wooden skewer inserted in the center comes out clean.
8. Remove the bread saucepan from oven and place onto a wire rack to cool for about 15 minutes.
9. Now, invert the bread onto the wire rack to cool completely before slicing.
10. Cut the bread loaf into desired-sized slices and serve.

Apple Bread

Servings|6   Time|10 minutes
Nutritional Content (per serving):
Cal| 240   Fat| 17.8g   Protein| 6.2g   Carbs| 16.8g   Fiber| 4.4g

Ingredients:

- Almond flour (1 cup)
- Baking soda (½ teaspoon)
- Ground cinnamon (½ teaspoon)
- Salt (¼ teaspoon)
- Maple syrup (2 tablespoons)
- Walnuts (¼ cup, chopped)
- Coconut flour (3 tablespoons)
- Baking soda (½ teaspoon)
- Ground cardamom (¼ teaspoon)
- Medium eggs (3)
- Medium apple (1, peeled, cored and chopped finely)

Directions:

1. Preheat your oven to 350 degrees F. Line a bread loaf saucepan with lightly greased parchment paper.
2. Place flours, baking soda, spices and salt in a bowl and mix well.
3. In a separate bowl, place eggs, oil and maple syrup and beat until well combined.
4. Add egg mixture into the bowl of flour mixture and mix until well combined.
5. Gently fold in apple pieces and walnuts.
6. Place the mixture into the prepared loaf saucepan.
7. Bake for approximately 30-40 minutes or until a wooden skewer inserted in the center comes out clean.
8. Remove the bread saucepan from oven and place onto a wire rack to cool for about 10 minutes.
9. Now, invert the bread onto the wire rack to cool completely before serving.
10. Cut the bread loaf in desired-sized slices and serve.

Quinoa Bread

Servings|12   Time|1½ hours
Nutritional Content (per serving):
Cal| 151   Fat| 7.2g   Protein| 4.5g   Carbs| 18.3g   Fiber| 3.8g

Ingredients:

- Uncooked quinoa (1¾, cups)
- Bicarbonate soda (½ teaspoon)
- Fresh lemon juice (1 tablespoon)
- Chia seeds (¼ cup)
- Salt, as required
- Olive oil (¼ cup)
- Water (½ cup)

Directions:

1. In a bowl, soak the quinoa in water overnight.
2. In another bowl, soak chia seeds in ½ cup of water overnight
3. Drain the quinoa and then rinse well.
4. Again, drain the quinoa.
5. Preheat your oven to 320 degrees F. Line a loaf saucepan with parchment paper.
6. Add all the ingredients in a food processor and pulse for about 3 minutes.
7. Place the mixture into the prepared loaf saucepan evenly.
8. Bake for approximately 1½ hours or until a toothpick inserted in the center comes out clean.
9. Remove it from the oven and place the loaf saucepan onto a wire rack to cool for at least 10-15 minutes.
10. Then invert the bread onto the rack to cool completely before slicing.
11. Cut the bread loaf into desired-sized slices and serve.

Lentil Goat Cheese Toasts

Servings|2 Time|10 minutes
Nutritional Content (per serving):
Cal| 384   Fat| 8.6g   Protein| 25g   Carbs| 54.9g   Fiber| 24.1g

Ingredients:

- ❖ Goat cheese (2 tablespoons)
- ❖ Canned green lentils (¾ cup, rinsed and drained)
- ❖ Fresh parsley (1 teaspoon, chopped)
- ❖ Whole-wheat bread slices (2, toasted)
- ❖ Walnuts (2 tablespoons, chopped)

Directions:

1. Arrange 1 bread slice onto each serving plate.
2. Place cheese over each slice evenly and then top with lentils and walnuts.
3. Garnish with parsley and serve.

Chickpeas Toasts

Servings|2   Time|17 minutes
Nutritional Content (per serving):

Cal| 620   Fat| 32.9g   Protein| 5.8g   Carbs| 68.9g   Fiber| 15.8g

Ingredients:

- Olive oil 1½ tablespoons, divided
- Ground turmeric (1 teaspoon)
- (Fresh lemon juice (1 teaspoon)
- Avocado (1, peeled, pitted and chopped roughly)
- Fresh parsley (1 teaspoon, chopped)

- Chickpeas (1 (16-ounce) can, rinsed, drained and pat dried)
- Salt and ground black pepper, as required
- Whole-wheat bread slices (2, toasted)

Directions:

1. In a wok, heat 1 tablespoon of oil over medium heat and cook the chickpeas for about 3-4 minutes, stirring continuously.
2. Stir in the turmeric and cooking for about 2-3 minutes or until chickpeas are toasted.
3. Remove from the heat and stir in the lemon juice, salt and black pepper. Set aside.
4. In a bowl, add the chopped avocado with a pinch of salt and black pepper and with a fork, mash well.
5. Arrange 1 bread slice onto each serving plate.
6. Spread mashed avocado on one side of each bread slice and top with chickpeas.
7. Garnish with parsley and serve.

Nuts Granola

Servings|8   Time|43 minutes
Nutritional Content (per serving):
Cal| 382   Fat| 25g   Protein| 7.3g   Carbs| 37.9g   Fiber| 3.5g

Ingredients:

- Unsweetened coconut flakes (½ cup)
- Raw sunflower seeds (¼ cup, shelled)
- Coconut oil (¼ cup)
- Vanilla extract (1 teaspoon)
- Raw almonds (1 cup)
- Raw cashews (1 cup)
- Raw pumpkin seeds (¼ cup, shelled)
- Maple syrup (½ cup)
- raisins (1 cup)

Directions:

1. Preheat your oven to 275 F. Line a large baking sheet with parchment paper.
2. In a food processor, add the coconut flakes, almonds, cashews, and seeds and pulse until chopped finely.
3. Meanwhile, in a medium non-stick saucepan, add the oil, maple syrup, and vanilla extract and cook for 3 minutes over medium-high heat, stirring continuously.
4. Remove from the heat and immediately stir in the nut mixture.
5. Transfer the mixture to the prepared baking sheet and spread it out evenly.
6. Bake for approximately 25 minutes, stirring twice.
7. Remove the saucepan from the oven and immediately stir in the raisins.
8. With the back of a spatula, flatten the surface of the mixture.
9. Set aside to cool completely.
10. Then, break into even chunks.
11. Serve with your choice of non-dairy milk and fruit topping.

Oats Granola

Servings|8   Time|48 minutes
Nutritional Content (per serving):
Cal| 169   Fat| 7.9g   Protein| 3.8g   Carbs| 23.2g   Fiber| 4g

Ingredients:

- Cacao powder (¼ cup)
- Coconut oil (2 tablespoons, melted)
- Rolled oats (2 cups)
- Chia seeds (2 tablespoons)
- Maple syrup (¼ cup)
- Vanilla extract (½ teaspoon)
- Salt (1/8 teaspoon)
- Almonds (¼ cup, chopped roughly)

Directions:

1. Preheat your oven to 300 degrees F. Line a medium baking sheet with parchment paper.
2. In a medium saucepan, add the cacao powder, maple syrup, coconut oil, vanilla extract and salt and mix well.
3. Now, place the saucepan over medium heat and cook for about 2-3 minutes or until thick and syrupy, stirring continuously.
4. Remove from the heat and set aside.
5. In a large bowl, add the oats, almonds and chia seeds and mix well.
6. Add the syrup mixture and mix until well combined.
7. Transfer the granola mixture onto a prepared baking sheet and spread in an even layer.
8. Bake for approximately 35 minutes.
9. Remove from the oven and set aside for about 1 hour.

Lunch Recipes

Chicken & Berries Salad

Servings|10   Time|31 minutes
Nutritional Content (per serving):
Cal| 335   Fat| 22.8g   Protein| 23.5g   Carbs| 12.5g   Fiber| 5.8g

Ingredients:

- Boneless, skinless chicken breasts (2 pounds)
- Garlic clove (1, minced)
- Fresh strawberries (2 cups, hulled and sliced)
- Fresh raspberries (1½ cups)
- Fresh spinach (10 cups, torn)
- Pecans (½ cup, chopped)
- Olive oil (½ cup)
- Fresh lemon juice (¼ cup)
- Salt and ground black pepper, as required
- Fresh blueberries (1½ cups)
- Large avocados (2, peeled, pitted and sliced)

Directions:

1. For marinade: in a large bowl, add oil, lemon juice, garlic, salt and black pepper and beat until well combined.
2. In a large resealable plastic bag, place the chicken and ¾ cup of marinade.
3. Seal bag and shake to coat well.
4. Refrigerate overnight.
5. Cover the bowl of remaining marinade and refrigerate before serving.
6. Preheat the grill to medium heat. Grease the grill grate.
7. Remove the chicken from the bag and discard the marinade.
8. Place the chicken onto grill grate and grill, covered for about 5-8 minutes per side.
9. Remove chicken from grill and cut into bite-sized pieces.
10. In a large bowl, add the chicken pieces, berries, avocado and spinach and mix.
11. Place the reserved marinade and toss to coat.
12. Top with pecans and serve immediately.

Chicken & Greens Salad

Servings|4   Time|30 minutes
Nutritional Content (per serving):
Cal| 316   Fat| 15.8g   Protein| 30.4g   Carbs| 15g   Fiber| 1.9g

Ingredients:

For Chicken:

- ❖ Skinless, boneless chicken breasts (3 (6-ounce), pounded slightly)
- ❖ Orange zest (3 teaspoons, grated)
- ❖ Fresh orange juice (1/3 cup)
- ❖ Garlic cloves (4, minced)
- ❖ Maple syrup (2 tablespoons)
- ❖ Dried thyme (1½ teaspoons)
- ❖ Salt and ground black pepper, as required

For Salad:

- ❖ Fresh baby kale (3 cups)
- ❖ Fresh baby spinach (3 cups)
- ❖ Cherry tomatoes (2 cups, quartered)
- ❖ Extra-virgin olive oil (3 tablespoons)
- ❖ Fresh lemon juice (2 tablespoons)
- ❖ Salt and ground black pepper, as required

Directions:

1. For chicken: in a large bowl, all the ingredients and mix well.
2. Refrigerate to marinate for about 6-8 hours, flipping occasionally.
3. Preheat your oven to broiler. Arrange the oven rack about 6-inch away from heating element. Line a broiler saucepan with a piece of foil.
4. Remove the chicken breasts from bag and discard the marinade.
5. Arrange the chicken breasts onto the prepared saucepan in a single layer.
6. Broil for about for 15 minutes, flipping once halfway through.
7. Remove the chicken breasts from oven and place onto a cutting board for about 10 minutes.
8. Cut the chicken breasts into desired-sized slices.
9. For salad: in a bowl, add all ingredients alongside and toss to coat well.
10. Add chicken slices and stir to combine.

11. Serve immediately.

Chicken Taco Salad

Servings|6   Time|45 minutes
Nutritional Content (per serving):
Cal| 380   Fat| 16.1g   Protein| 26.3g   Carbs| 36.4g   Fiber| 9.6g

Ingredients:

- Boneless, skinless chicken breasts (4 (4-ounce), pounded slightly)
- Chicken broth (¾ cup)
- Cooked brown rice (1½ cups)
- Medium avocados (2, peeled, pitted and sliced)
- Fresh cilantro (¼ cup, chopped)
- Salt and ground black pepper, as required
- Olive oil (2 tablespoons)
- Cooked black beans (1½ cups)
- Frozen corn (1½ cups, thawed)
- Large tomatoes (2, chopped)
- Fresh spinach (4 cups, torn)

Directions:

1. Season the chicken breasts with salt and black pepper evenly.
2. In a large wok, heat the oil over medium heat and cook the chicken breasts for about 5 minutes.
3. Flip the chicken breast and to with the broth.
4. Cook, covered for about 7-10 minutes or until cooked through.
5. With a slotted spoon, transfer the chicken breast into a bowl and with 2 forks, shred the meat.
6. Add any remaining liquid from the saucepan into the shredded chicken and stir to combine.
7. Divide the shredded chicken into serving bowls and serve with the topping ingredients.

Steak & Peach Salad

Servings|6   Time|27 minutes
Nutritional Content (per serving):
Cal| 241   Fat| 12g   Protein| 24.1g   Carbs| 9.6g   Fiber| 2g

Ingredients:

- Fresh lemon juice (4 teaspoons, divided)
- Salt and ground black pepper, as required
- Fresh baby spinach (8 cups)
- Feta cheese (1/3 cup, crumbled)
- Extra-virgin olive oil (1½ tablespoons, divided)
- Flank steak (1 pound, trimmed)
- Maple syrup (1 teaspoon)
- Peaches (3, pitted and sliced thinly)

Directions:

1. In a large bowl, mix together 1 teaspoon of lemon juice, 1½ teaspoons of oil, salt and black pepper.
2. Add the steak and coat with mixture generously.
3. Heat a greased non-stick wok over medium-high heat and cook the steak for about 5-6 minutes per side.
4. Transfer the steak onto a cutting board and set aside for about 10 minutes before slicing.
5. Cut the beef steak into desired-sized slices diagonally across the grain.
6. In a large bowl, add the remaining lemon juice, oil, maple syrup, sea salt and black pepper and beat until well combined.
7. Add the spinach and toss to coat well.
8. Divide the spinach onto 4 serving plates.
9. Top with beef slices, peach slices and cheese evenly and serve.

Steak & Veggie Salad

Servings|4   Time|23 minutes
Nutritional Content (per serving):
Cal| 327   Fat| 19.6g   Protein| 26.1g   Carbs| 12.1g   Fiber| 2.2g

Ingredients:

- Olive oil (4 tablespoons, divided)
- Salt and ground black pepper, as required
- Carrot (½ cup, peeled and shredded)
- Radish (½ cup, sliced)
- Fresh baby kale (5 cups)
- Strip steaks (3 (4-ounce), trimmed)
- Fresh lemon juice (2 tablespoons)
- Cucumber (½ cup, peeled, seeded and sliced)
- Cherry tomatoes (½ cup, halved)

Directions:

1. For steak: in a large heavy-bottomed wok, heat 1½ tablespoons of oil over high heat and cook the steaks with salt and black pepper for about 3-4 minutes per side.
2. Transfer the steaks onto a cutting board for about 5 minutes before slicing.
3. For dressing: in a bowl, add remaining oil, lemon juice, salt and black pepper and beat until well combined.
4. For salad: in a salad bowl, place remaining ingredients and mix.
5. Cut the steaks into desired sized slices against the grain.
6. Place the salad onto each serving plate.
7. Top each plate with steak slices.
8. Drizzle with dressing and serve.

Pork & Mango Salad

Servings|6   Time|37 minutes
Nutritional Content (per serving):
Cal| 308   Fat| 14.6g   Protein| 23.1g   Carbs| 24.5g   Fiber| 6.8g

Ingredients:

- ❖ Fresh rosemary, chopped finely)
- ❖ Extra-virgin olive oil (3 tablespoons)
- ❖ Dijon mustard (1 teaspoon)
- ❖ Salt and ground black pepper, as required
- ❖ Fresh baby spinach (8 cups)
- ❖ Avocado (2, peeled, pitted and chopped)

- ❖ Garlic clove (1, minced)
- ❖ Balsamic vinegar (3 tablespoons)
- ❖ Fresh lemon juice (1½ tablespoons)
- ❖ Maple syrup (1 teaspoon)
- ❖ Pork tenderloin (1 pound, trimmed)
- ❖ Mango (2 cups, peeled, pitted and chopped)

Directions:

1. Preheat your oven to 400 degrees F. Grease a large rimmed baking sheet.
2. For dressing: in a large bowl, add the rosemary, garlic, vinegar, oil, lemon juice, mustard, maple syrup, salt and black pepper and beat until well combined.
3. Coat the pork tenderloin with 1 tablespoon of the dressing.
4. Reserve the remaining dressing.
5. In the bottom of the prepared baking sheet, arrange the pork tenderloin and sprinkle with the remaining salt and black pepper.
6. Bake for approximately 20-22 minutes.
7. Remove the baking sheet of pork tenderloin from oven and place onto a cutting board for about 5 minutes.
8. With a sharp knife, cut the tenderloin into desired-sized slices.
9. In the bowl of reserved dressing, add the lettuce, mango and avocado and toss to coat.
10. Divide the salad onto the serving plates and top with pork slices.
11. Serve immediately.

Salmon & Beans Salad

Servings|8   Time|22 minutes
Nutritional Content (per serving):
Cal| 333   Fat| 16.5g   Protein| 23.6g   Carbs| 25.7g   Fiber| 8.8g

Ingredients:

- Salmon fillets (4 (6-ounce), skin removed)
- Olive oil (6 tablespoons, divided)
- Cooked navy beans (3 cups)
- Tomatoes (3, chopped)
- Fresh parsley (¼ cup, minced)
- Ground cumin (½ teaspoon)
- Salt and ground black pepper, as required
- Large cucumbers (3, chopped)
- Large onion (1, sliced)
- Fresh lemon juice (¼ cup)

Directions:

1. Sprinkle the salmon fillets with cumin, salt and black pepper evenly.
2. In a large non-stick wok, heat 2 tablespoons of the oil over medium heat.
3. Place the salmon fillets, skin-side down and cook for about 3-4 minutes.
4. Carefully flip the side and cook for about 3 minutes.
5. Transfer the salmon fillets onto a cutting board.
6. Cut each fillet into bite-sized pieces.
7. Meanwhile, in a salad bowl, add remaining oil, salt, black pepper, beans, veggies and parsley and toss to coat well.
8. Top with salmon pieces and serve.

Tuna Salad

Servings|4   Time|15 minutes
Nutritional Content (per serving):
Cal| 274   Fat| 14.7g   Protein| 29.8g   Carbs| 7g   Fiber| 1.8g

Ingredients:

For Dressing:

- ❖ Fresh dill (2 tablespoons, minced)
- ❖ Olive oil (2 tablespoons)
- ❖ Fresh lemon juice (1 tablespoon)
- ❖ Salt and ground black pepper, to taste

For Salad:

- ❖ Water-packed tuna (2 (6-ounce) cans, drained and flaked)
- ❖ Fresh spinach (4 cups, torn)
- ❖ Hard-boiled eggs (6, peeled and sliced)
- ❖ Tomato (1 cup, chopped)
- ❖ Large cucumber (1, sliced)

Directions:

1. For dressing: place dill, oil, lime juice, salt, and black pepper in a small bowl and beat until well combined.
2. Divide the spinach onto serving plates and top each with tuna, egg, cucumber, and tomato.
3. Drizzle with dressing and serve.

Shrimp & Corn Salad

Servings|4   Time|25minutes
Nutritional Content (per serving):
Cal| 263   Fat| 12.7g   Protein| 22.1g   Carbs| 17g   Fiber| 3.2g

Ingredients:

For Shrimp:

- ❖ Olive oil (1 tablespoon)
- ❖ Shrimp (¾ pound, peeled and deveined)
- ❖ Garlic cloves (2, minced)
- ❖ Salt, as required
- ❖ Fresh lemon juice (1 tablespoon)

For Salad:

- ❖ Fresh spinach (4 cups, torn)
- ❖ Frozen corn (1 cup, thawed)
- ❖ Large tomatoes (2, chopped)
- ❖ Onion (1 cup, sliced)
- ❖ Olive oil (2 tablespoons)
- ❖ Salt and ground black pepper, as required

Directions:

1. In a medium wok, heat olive oil over medium-high heat and cook the shrimp for about 2 minutes.
2. Flip the shrimp and adjust the heat to medium-low.
3. Stir in the garlic and salt and cook for about 2-3 minutes.
4. Stir in lemon juice and remove from heat.
5. Set aside to cool completely.
6. In a large salad bowl, add shrimp and all salad ingredients and toss to coat well.
7. Serve immediately.

Shrimp & Veggie Salad

Servings|6   Time|18 minutes
Nutritional Content (per serving):
Cal| 276   Fat| 16.9g   Protein| 20.4g   Carbs| 13.1g   Fiber| 6g

Ingredients:

- ❖ Medium shrimp (1 pound)
- ❖ Large avocados (2, peeled, pitted and chopped)
- ❖ Onion (1 cup, chopped)
- ❖ Balsamic vinegar (2 tablespoons)
- ❖ Fresh cilantro (3 tablespoons, chopped)
- ❖ Lemon (1, quartered)
- ❖ Tomatoes (1½ cups, chopped)
- ❖ Cucumber (1½ cups, chopped
- ❖ Fresh baby spinach (8 cups)
- ❖ Extra-virgin olive oil (2 tablespoons)
- ❖ Garlic (1 teaspoon, minced)

Directions:

1. In a large saucepan of the salted boiling water, add the shrimp and lemon and cook for about 3 minutes.
2. Remove from the heat and drain the shrimp well.
3. Set aside to cool.
4. After cooling, peel and devein the shrimps.
5. Transfer the shrimp into a large bowl.
6. Add the remaining all ingredients and gently stir to combine.
7. Cover the bowl and refrigerate for about 1 hour before serving.

Scallops & Strawberry Salad

Servings|6   Time|22 minutes
Nutritional Content (per serving):
Cal| 263   Fat| 12.1g   Protein| 20.3g   Carbs| 20.2g   Fiber| 3g

Ingredients:

For Scallops:

- ❖ Sea scallops (1¼ pounds, side muscles removed)
- ❖ Salt and ground black pepper, as required
- ❖ Extra-virgin olive oil (2 tablespoons)
- ❖ Garlic clove (1, minced)
- ❖ Fresh rosemary (1 tablespoon, minced)

For Salad:

- ❖ Fresh baby kale (8 cups)
- ❖ Fresh strawberries (3 cups, hulled and sliced)
- ❖ Olive oil (2 tablespoons)
- ❖ Fresh lime juice (2 tablespoons)
- ❖ Salt and ground black pepper, as required
- ❖ Feta cheese (1/3 cup, crumbled)

Directions:

1. Sprinkle the scallops with salt and black pepper evenly.
2. In a large wok, heat the oil over medium-high heat and sauté the garlic and rosemary for about 1 minute.
3. Add the scallops and cook for about 2-3 minutes per side.
4. Meanwhile, for salad: in a bowl, add all ingredients and toss to coat well.
5. Divide the salad onto serving plates.
6. Top each plate with scallops and serve.

Scallops & Egg Salad

Servings|8   Time|20 minutes
Nutritional Content (per serving):
Cal| 268   Fat| 11.3g   Protein| 24g   Carbs| 18.8g   Fiber| 2.8g

Ingredients:

- Olive oil (2 tablespoons)
- Salt and ground black pepper, as required
- Dijon mustard (3 tablespoons)
- Large apples (2, cored and sliced)
- Walnuts (¼ cup, chopped)
- Sea scallops (1½ pounds, side muscles removed)
- Plain Greek yogurt (¼ cup)
- Hard-boiled eggs (8, peeled and sliced)
- Fresh baby kale (8 cups)

Directions:

1. In a large non-stick wok, heat the olive oil over medium-high heat.
2. Stir in the scallops, salt and black pepper and immediately adjust the heat to high.
3. Cook for about 5 minutes, flipping once halfway through.
4. Transfer the scallops into a bowl and set aside to cool.
5. For dressing: in a bowl, add yogurt and mustard and beat until well combined.
6. For salad: in a large serving bowl, add remaining ingredients and mix.
7. Top with scallops and drizzle with dressing.
8. Serve immediately.

Chickpeas & Kale Salad

Servings|3   Time|18 minutes
Nutritional Content (per serving):
Cal| 353   Fat| 14.8g   Protein| 13.9g   Carbs| 45.22g   Fiber| 7.8g

Ingredients:

- Olive oil (1 teaspoon)
- Fresh kale (2 cups, tough ribs removed and torn)
- Hemp seeds (2 tablespoons)
- Fresh lemon juice (1 tablespoon)
- Dijon mustard (½ teaspoon)
- Chickpeas (1 (14-ounce)
- Cashews (½ cup, soaked and drained)
- Small garlic clove (1, peeled)
- Capers (1 teaspoon)
- Salt and ground black pepper, as required

Directions:

1. For salad: in a non-stick wok, heat the oil over medium-low heat and cook the chickpeas for about 2-3 minutes, stirring frequently.
2. Remove from the heat and transfer the chickpeas into a bowl. Set aside to cool.
3. Meanwhile, for dressing: in a blender, add all the ingredients except for kale and pulse until smooth.
4. In the bowl of chickpeas, add the kale and dressing and toss to coat well.
5. Serve immediately.

Quinoa & Veggie Salad

Servings|6   Time|35 minutes
Nutritional Content (per serving):
Cal| 200   Fat| 9.1g   Protein| 5.5g   Carbs| 26g   Fiber| 4.1g

Ingredients:

- Water (2 cups)
- Salt, as required
- Bell peppers (1 cup, seeded and chopped)
- Fresh baby greens (6 cups)
- Apple cider vinegar (2 tablespoons)
- Quinoa (1 cup, rinsed)
- Cherry tomatoes (1 cup, halved)
- Black olives (1 cup, pitted)
- Frozen corn (½ cup, thawed)
- Olive oil (2 tablespoons)
- Fresh ginger (1 tablespoon, minced finely)

Directions:

1. In a saucepan, add water, quinoa and salt and bring to a boil on high heat.
2. Adjust the heat to low and simmer, covered for about 15 minutes or until the liquid is absorbed.
3. Transfer the quinoa into a large salad bowl.
4. Set aside to cool.
5. In the bowl of quinoa, add remaining ingredients and mix until well combined.
6. Serve immediately.

Chicken Stuffed Avocado

Servings|2   Time|15 minutes
Nutritional Content (per serving):
Cal| 280   Fat| 20.8g   Protein| 13.6g   Carbs| 12.4g   Fiber| 7.2g

Ingredients:

- Cooked chicken (½ cup, shredded)
- Onion (¼ cup, chopped finely)
- Salt and ground black pepper, as required
- Avocado (1, halved and pitted)
- Fresh lime juice (1 tablespoon)
- Plain Greek yogurt (¼ cup)
- Dijon mustard (1 teaspoon)
- Pinch of cayenne pepper

Directions:

1. With a spoon, scoop out the flesh from the middle of each avocado half and transfer into a bowl.
2. Add the lime juice and mash until well combined.
3. Add remaining ingredients and stir to combine.
4. Divide the chicken mixture in avocado halves evenly and serve immediately.

Tuna Stuffed Avocados

Servings|2   Time|15 minutes
Nutritional Content (per serving):
Cal| 396   Fat| 32.3g   Protein| 2.4g   Carbs| 19.9g   Fiber| 5.9g

Ingredients:

- ❖ 1 Large avocado (1, halved and pitted)
- ❖ Fresh lemon juice (2 tablespoons)
- ❖ Salt and ground black pepper, as required
- ❖ Water-packed tuna (1 (5-ounce) can, drained and flaked)
- ❖ Mayonnaise (3 tablespoons)
- ❖ Onion (1 tablespoon, chopped finely)

Directions:

1. Carefully remove abut about 2-3 tablespoons of flesh from each avocado half.
2. Arrange the avocado halves onto a platter and drizzle each with 1 teaspoon of lemon juice.
3. Chop the avocado flesh and transfer into a bowl.
4. In the bowl of avocado flesh, add tuna, mayonnaise, onion, remaining lemon juice, salt, and black pepper, and stir to combine.
5. Divide the tuna mixture in both avocado halves evenly.
6. Serve immediately.

Chicken Pita Sandwiches

Servings|4   Time|28 minutes
Nutritional Content (per serving):
Cal| 273   Fat| 7.5g   Protein| 28.5g   Carbs| 23.7g   Fiber| 4.1g

Ingredients:

For Chicken Marinade:

- Fresh lemon juice (2 tablespoons)
- Olive oil (3 teaspoons)
- Garlic (1½ teaspoons, minced)
- Lemon zest (1 teaspoon, grated)
- Salt and ground black pepper, as required
- Chicken tenders (1 pound)

For Sandwiches:

- Whole-wheat pita breads (2 (6½-inch), halved)
- Fresh spinach (1 cup, torn)
- Tomatoes(1 cup, chopped)
- English cucumber (½, chopped)
- Red onion (½ cup, sliced)

Directions:

1. For marinade: in a large ceramic bowl, add all ingredients except for chicken and mix well.
2. Add chicken tenders and toss to coat.
3. Cover the bowl and refrigerate to marinate for about 2 hours.
4. Preheat the grill to medium-high heat. Lightly, grease the grill grate.
5. Remove the chicken tenders from the bowl and shake off excess marinade.
6. Place the chicken tenders onto the grill and cook for about 3-4 minutes per side.
7. Fill each pita half with chicken, spinach, tomato, cumber and onion.
8. Serve immediately.

Beef & Mango Tortillas

Servings|4   Time|15 minutes
Nutritional Content (per serving):
Cal| 296   Fat| 13.1g   Protein| 26.8g   Carbs| 18.3g   Fiber| 2.8g

Ingredients:

- ❖ Fresh lime juice (2 tablespoons)
- ❖ Dijon mustard (1 tablespoon)
- ❖ Cooked beef (2 cups, shredded)
- ❖ Mango (1 cup, peeled, pitted and cubed)
- ❖ Fresh cilantro (¼ cup, chopped)
- ❖ Olive oil (2 tablespoons)
- ❖ Salt and ground black pepper, as required
- ❖ Fresh kale (1 cup, tough ribs removed and chopped)
- ❖ Whole-wheat tortillas (4 (10-inch), warmed)

Directions:

1. In a large bowl, add mustard, lime juice, oil and black pepper and beat until well combined.
2. Add beef, mango, cabbage and cilantro and toss to coat well.
3. Arrange the tortillas onto a smooth surface.
4. Place beef mixture over each tortilla, leaving about 1-inch border all around.
5. Carefully fold the edges of each tortilla over the filling to roll up.
6. Cut each roll in half cross-wise and serve.

Beef Burgers

Servings|6 Time|35 minutes
Nutritional Content (per serving):
Cal| 239   Fat| 12g   Protein| 25g   Carbs| 8.2g   Fiber| 2.6g

Ingredients:

- Ground beef (1 pound)
- Medium beetroot (1, trimmed, peeled and chopped finely)
- Serrano peppers (2, seeded and chopped)
- Salt and ground black pepper, as required
- Fresh baby spinach (6 cups)
- Carrot (1, peeled and chopped finely)
- Small onion (1, chopped finely)
- Fresh cilantro (1 tablespoon, chopped finely)
- Olive oil (3 tablespoons)
- Tomatoes (4, sliced)

Directions:

1. In
2. For patties: in a large bowl, add all ingredients except for oil and mix until well combined.
3. Make equal-sized 6 patties from mixture.
4. In a large non-stick wok, heat the olive oil over medium heat and cook the patties in 2 batches for about 4-5 minutes per side or until golden brown.
5. Divide the tomato and spinach onto serving plates
6. Top each with 1 patty and serve.

Salmon Burgers

Servings|4   Time|35 minutes
Nutritional Content (per serving):
Cal| 316   Fat| 13g   Protein| 24.9g   Carbs| 25.5g   Fiber| 3.3g

Ingredients:

- Olive oil (1 teaspoon)
- Shallots (1/3 cup, chopped finely)
- Skinless salmon fillets (16 ounces)
- Dijon mustard (2 tablespoons)
- Fresh baby greens (5 cups)
- Fresh kale (1 cup, tough ribs removed and chopped)
- Salt and ground black pepper, as required
- Cooked quinoa (¾ cup)
- Large egg (1, beaten)
- Cucumber (2 cups, chopped)

Directions:

1. For burgers: in a large non-stick wok, heat the oil over medium heat and sauté the kale, shallot and kale, salt and black pepper for about 4-5 minutes.
2. Remove from heat and transfer the kale mixture into a large bowl.
3. Set aside to cool slightly.
4. With a knife, chop 4 ounces of salmon and transfer into the bowl of kale mixture.
5. In a food processor, add the remaining salmon and pulse until finely chopped.
6. Transfer the finely chopped salmon into the bowl of kale mixture.
7. Then, add remaining ingredients except for baby greens and cucumber and stir until fully combined.
8. Make 5 equal-sized patties from the mixture.
9. Heat a lightly greased large non-stick wok over medium heat and cook the patties for about 4-5 minutes per side.
10. Divide the baby greens and cucumber onto serving plates and top each with 1 patty.
11. Serve immediately.

Tuna Burgers

Servings|2   Time|21 minutes
Nutritional Content (per serving):
Cal| 442   Fat| 20.8g   Protein| 54.1g   Carbs| 9.4g   Fiber| 2.4g

Ingredients:

- ❖ Water packed tuna (1 (15-ounce) can, drained)
- ❖ Fresh dill (1 teaspoon, chopped)
- ❖ Walnuts (2 tablespoons, chopped)
- ❖ Small carrot (1, peeled and chopped)
- ❖ Celery stalk (½, chopped)
- ❖ Fresh parsley (2 tablespoons, chopped)
- ❖ Mayonnaise (2 tablespoons)
- ❖ Egg (1, beaten)
- ❖ Olive oil (1 tablespoon)
- ❖ Fresh baby spinach (3 cups)

Directions:

1. For burgers: in a bowl, add all ingredients except for oil, spinach and acrrot and mix until well combined.
2. Make 2 equal-sized patties from mixture.
3. In a frying saucepan, heat oil over medium heat and cook the patties for about 2-3 minutes per side.
4. Divide the lettuce onto serving plates.
5. Top each plate with 1 burger and serve.

Chickpeas Burgers

Servings|4   Time|30 minutes
Nutritional Content (per serving):
Cal| 326   Fat| 7.1g   Protein| 12.9g   Carbs| 45.6g   Fiber| 9g

Ingredients:

- Water (1 cup)
- Broccoli florets 1½ cups)
- Onion (½ cup, chopped)
- Ground cumin (2 teaspoons)
- Tahini (1 tablespoon)
- Saucepanko breadcrumbs ½ cup)
- Fresh baby kale (4 cups)
- Dry couscous (1/3 cup)
- Olive oil (2 teaspoons)
- Scallion (½ cup, chopped)
- Ground turmeric (¼ teaspoon)
- Chickpeas (1 (15-ounce) can, rinsed and drained)
- Tomatoes (1 cup, chopped)

Directions:

1. Preheat your oven to 400 degrees F. Line a baking sheet with foil paper.
2. In a small saucepan, mix together water and couscous over medium heat and bring to a boil.
3. Immediately remove from heat and set aside, covered for about 10 minutes or until all the liquid is absorbed.
4. Meanwhile, in a saucepan of boiling water, cook the broccoli for about 5-7 minutes.
5. Drain the broccoli well.
6. Meanwhile, in a wok, heat the oil over medium heat and sauté the onion and scallion for about 3-5 minutes.
7. Stir in the cumin and turmeric and remove from heat.
8. In a food processor, add the couscous, broccoli, onion mixture, tahini and chickpeas and pulse until well combined.
9. Transfer the mixture into a bowl with breadcrumbs and stir to combine.
10. Make equal-sized patties from mixture.
11. Arrange the patties onto the prepared baking sheet in a single layer.
12. Bake for approximately 50 minutes, flipping once halfway through.
13. Divide kale and tomato onto serving plates.

14. Top each plate with 1 patty and serve.

Beans & Quinoa Burgers

Servings|4   Time|1¼ hours
Nutritional Content (per serving):
Cal| 322   Fat| 3.7g   Protein| 7.1g   Carbs| 58g   Fiber| 14.9g

Ingredients:

- Quinoa (½ cup, rinsed)
- Dried thyme (3 teaspoons, divided)
- Flaxseed meal (1 tablespoon)
- Fresh corn (½ cup)
- Oat flour (1/3 cup)
- Shallot (½ cup, chopped finely)
- Fresh lime juice (2 tablespoons)
- Smoked paprika (½ teaspoon)
- Fresh baby kale (6 cups)
- Water (1 cup plus 3 tablespoons, divided)
- Garlic powder (1 teaspoon)
- Black beans (1 (15-ounces) can, drained and rinsed)
- Bell pepper (½ cup, seeded and chopped finely)
- Salt and ground black pepper, as required
- Cucumbers (2, sliced)

Directions:

1. Preheat your oven to 375 degrees F. Line a baking sheet with greased parchment paper.
2. For patties: in a medium saucepan, add 1 cup of the water, quinoa, 1 teaspoon of thyme and garlic powder over medium-high heat and bring to a boil.
3. Adjust the heat to low and simmer, covered for about 15 minutes.
4. Remove from the heat and set aside, covered for about 5-10 minutes.
5. In a small bowl, add the remaining water and flaxseed and mix well. Set aside for about 5 minutes.
6. In a large bowl, add ¾ of the beans and with a fork, mash them.
7. Add the remaining beans, flaxseed mixture, quinoa, corn, oat flour, bell pepper, shallots, lemon juice, remaining thyme, paprika, salt and black pepper and mix until well combined.
8. Make equal-sized patties from the mixture.
9. Arrange the patties onto the prepared baking sheet in a single layer.
10. Bake for approximately 15 minutes per side.

11. Divide the kale, cucumber and patties onto serving plates and serve.

Lentil Burgers

Servings|3   Time|30 minutes
Nutritional Content (per serving):
Cal| 266   Fat| 17.5g   Protein| 7.6g   Carbs| 23.3g   Fiber| 7.8g

Ingredients:

- ❖ Chickpea lentils (1 cup)
- ❖ Green chilies (2, chopped finely)
- ❖ Pinch of ground turmeric
- ❖ Olive oil (¼ cup)
- ❖ Fresh baby spinach (4 cups)
- ❖ Onion (1 cup, chopped finely)
- ❖ Garlic paste (1 teaspoon)
- ❖ Ginger paste (1 teaspoon)
- ❖ Salt, as required
- ❖ Tomatoes (2, chopped)

Directions:

1. In a bowl of water, soak the chickpea lentil for at least 3-4 hours.
2. Drain the lentils and rinse under cold running water.
3. Through a strainer, strain the lentils completely.
4. In the bowl of a food processor, place lentils and pulse until a coarse paste is formed.
5. Transfer the lentils into a bowl.
6. Add the onion, green chilies, garlic paste, ginger paste, turmeric and salt and mix until well combined.
7. Make small equal-sized patties from the mixture.
8. In a wok, heat olive oil over medium heat and cook half of the patties for 5 minutes, flipping occasionally.
9. Divide the tomato and spinach onto serving plates and top each with patties.
10. Serve immediately.

Chicken Meatballs

Servings|4   Time|30 minutes
Nutritional Content (per serving):
Cal| 347   Fat| 22g   Protein| 30.9g   Carbs| 3.9g   Fiber| 1.8g

Ingredients:

- ❖ Ground chicken (1 pound)
- ❖ Large egg (1, beaten)
- ❖ Fresh parsley (2 tablespoons, chopped)
- ❖ Olive oil (2 tablespoons)
- ❖ Black olives (1 cup, pitted)
- ❖ Garlic cloves (2, minced)
- ❖ Parmesan cheese (½ cup, grated)
- ❖ Salt and ground black pepper, as required
- ❖ Fresh baby spinach (4 cups)

Directions:

1. For meatballs: in a large bowl, add all ingredients except for oil, olives and spinach and with your hands, mix until well combined.
2. Make small equal-sized balls from the mixture.
3. In a non-stick wok, heat oil over medium heat and cook the meatballs for about 10 minutes or until done completely.
4. With a slotted spoon, transfer the meatballs onto a paper towel-lined plate to drain.
5. Divide the meatballs, olives, spinach and lemon slices onto serving plates and serve immediately.

Meatballs with Sweet Potato

Servings|4   Time|10 minutes
Nutritional Content (per serving):
Cal| 365   Fat| 22.8g   Protein| 26.5g   Carbs| 15.1g   Fiber| 2.5g

Ingredients:

- Sweet potatoes (2, peeled and cubed)
- Salt and ground black pepper, as required
- Feta cheese (½ cup, crumbled)
- Dried oregano (½ teaspoon)
- Olive oil (4 tablespoons, divided)
- Lean ground turkey (1 pound)
- Frozen chopped spinach (1 cup, thawed and squeezed)

Directions:

1. Preheat your oven to 400 degrees F. Line a large baking sheet with parchment paper.
2. For sweet potatoes: in a large bowl, add the sweet potato cubes and 2 tablespoons of oil and toss to coat well.
3. Place the sweet potato cubes onto the prepared baking sheet in a single layer.
4. Bake for approximately 25-30 minutes, flipping once halfway through.
5. Remove the baking sheet from oven and set aside to cool.
6. Meanwhile, for meatballs: place all ingredients except for oil in a bowl and mix until well combined.
7. Make 12 equal-sized meatballs form the mixture.
8. Heat the olive oil in a large non-stick wok over medium heat and cook the meatballs for about 10-15 minutes or until done completely, flipping occasionally.
9. With a slotted spoon, transfer the meatballs onto a plate
10. Drain the broccoli and transfer into a bowl.
11. Divide meatballs and sweet potato onto serving plates and serve.

Meatballs Kabobs

Servings|6   Time|29 minutes
Nutritional Content (per serving):
Cal| 201   Fat| 8.9g   Protein| 23.3g   Carbs| 7.7g   Fiber| 1.4g

Ingredients:

- Onion (1, chopped roughly)
- Garlic cloves (2, chopped roughly)
- Sesame oil (1 teaspoon)
- Low-sodium soy sauce (½ tablespoon)
- Medium carrots (2, peeled and chopped)
- Lemongrass (½ cup, chopped roughly)
- Lean ground turkey (1½ pounds)
- Arrowroot starch (1 tablespoon)
- Salt and ground black pepper, as required
- Fresh baby greens (6 cups)

Directions:

1. Preheat the grill to medium-high heat. Grease the grill grate.
2. In a food processor, add the onion, lemongrass and garlic and pulse until chopped finely.
3. Transfer the onion mixture into a large bowl.
4. Add the remaining ingredients and mix until well combined.
5. Make 12 equal-sized balls from the meat mixture.
6. Thread the balls onto the presoaked wooden skewers.
7. Place the skewers onto the grill and cook for about 6-7 minutes per side.
8. Serve hot alongside the carrots and baby greens.

Kale & Carrot Soup

Servings|5   Time|55 minutes
Nutritional Content (per serving):
Cal| 140   Fat| 6.9g   Protein| 6.6g   Carbs| 13.8g   Fiber| 2.7g

Ingredients:

- Olive oil (2 tablespoons)
- Celery stalks (2, chopped)
- Garlic cloves (2, crushed)
- Salt and ground black pepper, as required
- Vegetable broth (4½ cups)
- Medium carrots (4, chopped)
- Large onion (1, chopped finely)
- Fresh kale (½ pound, tough ribs removed and chopped finely)

Directions:

1. Heat the oil in a large soup saucepan over medium heat and cook the carrot, celery, onion and garlic for about 8-10 minutes, stirring frequently.
2. Add the kale and cook for about 5 minutes, stirring twice.
3. Add the broth and bring to a boil.
4. Cook partially covered for about 20 minutes.
5. Stir in salt and black pepper and remove from the heat.
6. With an immersion blender, blend the soup until smooth.
7. Serve hot.

Spinach & Broccoli Soup

Servings|3   Time|35 minutes
Nutritional Content (per serving):
Cal| 135   Fat| 9.2g   Protein| 6.5g   Carbs| 10.5g   Fiber| 4.5g

Ingredients:

- Olive oil (1 tablespoon)
- Garlic cloves (3-4, chopped)
- Celery stalks (2, chopped)
- Green chilies (1-2, chopped)
- Vegetable broth (1½ cups)
- Fresh spinach (3 cups)
- Chia seeds (2 tablespoons)
- Onion (¼ cup), chopped
- Broccoli (2 cups, cut into small pieces)
- Salt, as required
- Unsweetened almond milk (1½ cups)
- Fresh lemon juice (1 teaspoon)

Directions:

1. Heat olive oil in a saucepan over medium heat and sauté the onion and garlic for about 4-5 minutes.
2. Add the broccoli, celery, green chilies, salt, broth and milk and stir to combine.
3. Increase the heat to medium-high and bring to a boil.
4. Adjust the heat to medium-low and cook for about 10 minutes.
5. Add spinach and chia seeds and cook for about 1-2 minutes.
6. Remove the saucepan of soup from heat and with an immersion blender, blend until smooth.
7. Drizzle with lemon juice and serve hot.

Tofu & Spinach Soup

Servings|4   Time|50 minutes
Nutritional Content (per serving):
Cal| 132   Fat| 7.7g   Protein| 11.3g   Carbs| 5.5g   Fiber| 1.6g

Ingredients:

- ❖ Olive oil (1 tablespoon)
- ❖ Garlic cloves (3, sliced)
- ❖ Sriracha (1 tablespoon)
- ❖ Fresh baby spinach (5 ounces)
- ❖ Firm tofu (1 cup, pressed, drained and cut into ½-inch cubes)
- ❖ Onion (¼ cup, sliced thinly)
- ❖ Vegetable broth (4 cups)
- ❖ Lemongrass (1 (4-inch) piece, sliced and smashed)
- ❖ Fresh cilantro (1 tablespoon, chopped)
- ❖ Fresh lime juice (3 tablespoons)

Directions:

1. In a heavy large saucepan, heat the oil over medium-low heat and cook the onions, garlic, and a little salt for about 15 minutes, stirring occasionally.
2. Stir in the broth, Leaping Sriracha, and lemongrass, and cover the saucepan.
3. Increase the heat to high and bring to a boil.
4. Remove from the heat and set aside, covered for about 15 minutes.
5. Uncover the saucepan and discard lemongrass.
6. In the saucepan, add the spinach, tofu, cilantro and lime juice, and stir to combine.
7. Place the saucepan over medium heat and cook for about 3-4 minutes, stirring occasionally.
8. Stir in the salt and serve hot.

Tofu with Kale & Chickpeas

Servings|4   Time|50 minutes
Nutritional Content (per serving):
Cal| 317   Fat| 1.3g   Protein| 14.2g   Carbs| 36.7g   Fiber| 7.1g

Ingredients:

For Tofu:

- ❖ Olive oil (2 tablespoons)
- ❖ Tofu (16 ounces, pressed, drained and cubed)
- ❖ Low-sodium soy sauce (1 tablespoon)
- ❖ Maple syrup (1 teaspoon)
- ❖ Water (¼ cup)

For Chickpeas & Kale:

- ❖ Olive oil (2 tablespoons)
- ❖ Canned chickpeas (3 cups, rinsed and drained)
- ❖ Ground turmeric (¼ teaspoon)
- ❖ Salt and ground black pepper, as required
- ❖ Fresh baby kale (6 cups)

Directions:

1. For tofu: in a large cast-iron wok, heat the olive oil over medium heat and cook the tofu cubes for about 8-10 minutes or until golden from all sides.
2. Add the remaining ingredients and cook for about 2-3 minutes.
3. Meanwhile, for chickpeas mixture: in another wok, heat the oil over medium heat and cook the chickpeas, turmeric, salt and black pepper for about 2-3 minutes.
4. Remove the chickpeas from heat and transfer into a large bowl.
5. Add the tofu mixture and kale and stir to combine.
6. Serve immediately.

Tofu with Spinach

Servings|2 Time|25 minutes
Nutritional Content (per serving):
Cal| 180   Fat| 11.8g   Protein| 12.1g   Carbs| 10.6g   Fiber| 1.5g

Ingredients:

- Extra-virgin olive oil (1 tablespoon)
- Fresh ginger (1 teaspoon, minced)
- Fresh spinach (6 ounces, chopped)
- Tofu (½ pound, pressed, drained and cubed)
- Garlic clove (1, minced)
- Red pepper flakes (¼ teaspoon)
- Low-sodium soy sauce (1 tablespoon)

Directions:

1. Heat the olive oil in a large non-stick wok over medium-high heat and stir-fry the tofu for about 3-3 minutes.
2. Add the ginger, garlic and red pepper flakes and cook for about 1 minute, stirring continuously.
3. Stir in the kale and soy sauce and stir-fry for about 4-5 minutes.
4. Serve hot.

Shrimp with Green Beans

Servings|4   Time|28 minutes
Nutritional Content (per serving):
Cal| 253   Fat| 12.7g   Protein| 28.7g   Carbs| 7.1g   Fiber| 2.5g

Ingredients:

- Olive oil (3 tablespoons)
- Fresh green beans (¾ pound, trimmed)
- Garlic (1 teaspoon, minced)
- Fresh ginger (1 teaspoon, minced)
- Fresh lime juice (2 tablespoons)
- Shrimp (1 pound, peeled and deveined)
- Salt and ground black pepper, as required
- Low-sodium soy sauce (1 tablespoon)

Directions:

1. In a wok, heat 2 tablespoons of oil over medium-high heat and cook the shrimp with salt and black pepper for about 3-4 minutes.
2. With a slotted spoon, transfer the shrimp into a bowl. Set aside.
3. In the same wok, heat remaining 1 tablespoon of oil over medium-high heat and cook the green beans, ginger, garlic, salt and black pepper for about 6-8 minutes, stirring frequently.
4. Stir in the shrimp and soy sauce and cook for about 1 minute.
5. Stir in the lemon juice and serve hot.

Prawns with Kale

Servings|4   Time|35 minutes
Nutritional Content (per serving):
Cal| 303   Fat| 12.5g   Protein| 30.4g   Carbs| 18.6g   Fiber| 2.5g

Ingredients:

- Prawns (1 pound, peeled and deveined)
- Onion (1, chopped finely)
- Fresh red chili (1, sliced)
- Low-sodium soy sauce (3 tablespoons)
- Orange zest (1 tablespoon, grated finely)
- Ground black pepper, as required
- Salt, as required
- Extra-virgin olive oil (3 tablespoons, divided)
- Fresh kale (1 pound, tough ribs removed and chopped)
- Fresh orange juice (3 tablespoons)
- Red pepper flakes (½ teaspoon, crushed)

Directions:

1. Season the prawns with a little salt.
2. In a large non-stick wok, heat 2 tablespoons of olive oil over high heat and stir-fry the prawns for about 2-3 minutes.
3. With a slotted spoon, transfer the prawns onto a plate.
4. In the same wok, heat the remaining oil over medium heat and sauté the onion for about 4-5 minutes.
5. Add the kale and stir-fry for about 2-3 minutes.
6. With a lid, cover the saucepan and cook for about 2 minutes.
7. Add the soy sauce, orange juice, zest, red pepper flakes and black pepper and stir to combine well.
8. Stir in the cooked prawns and cook for about 2-3 minutes.
9. Serve hot.

Scallops with Broccoli

Servings|2 Time|24 minutes
Nutritional Content (per serving):
Cal| 220   Fat| 5.1g   Protein| 6.3g   Carbs| 90.6g   Fiber| 1.4g

Ingredients:

- Olive oil (2 tablespoons)
- Garlic clove (1, crushed)
- Scallops (½ pound)
- Salt, as required
- Broccoli (1 cup, cut into small pieces)
- Fresh lemon juice (1 teaspoon)

Directions:

1. Heat oil in a large wok over medium heat and cook the broccoli and garlic for about 3-4 minutes, stirring occasionally.
2. Add in the scallops and cook for about 3-4 minutes, flipping occasionally.
3. Stir in the lemon juice and remove from the heat.
4. Serve hot.

Dinner Recipes

Chicken & Kale Soup

Servings|4   Time|30 minutes
Nutritional Content (per serving):
Cal| 190   Fat| 9.5g   Protein| 17g   Carbs| 9g   Fiber| 1.2g

Ingredients:

- Extra-virgin olive oil (2 tablespoons)
- Chicken broth (4 cups)
- Fresh kale (1 bunch, tough ribs removed and chopped)
- Salt and ground black pepper, as required
- Medium onion (½, chopped)
- Garlic cloves (3, minced)
- Cooked chicken (1 cup, cubed)
- Fresh lemon juice (2 tablespoons)

Directions:

1. In a soup saucepan, heat olive oil over medium-high heat and sauté the onion and garlic for about 2-3 minutes.
2. Stir in the cooked chicken and broth and bring to a gentle boil.
3. Now, adjust the heat and to low and simmer for about 3 minutes.
4. Stir in the kale and simmer for 5 minutes or until kale is tender.
5. Stir in the lemon juice, salt and black pepper and remove from the heat.
6. Serve hot.

Turkey & Sweet Potato Soup

Servings|8 Time|1 hour
Nutritional Content (per serving):
Cal| 294   Fat| 10.1g   Protein| 22.1g   Carbs| 29.9g   Fiber| 5.6g

Ingredients:

- Olive oil (2 tablespoons)
- Carrots (2 cups, peeled and chopped)
- Lean ground turkey (1½ pounds)
- Red chili powder (3 teaspoons)
- Salt and ground black pepper, as required
- Yellow onion (1, chopped)
- Celery stalks (2, chopped)
- Garlic cloves (2, minced)
- Tomatoes (4 cups, crushed finely)
- Sweet potato (5 cups, peeled and cubed)
- Chicken broth (8 cups)

Directions:

1. In a large Dutch oven, heat the olive oil over medium heat and sauté the onions and carrot for about 3 minutes.
2. Add the garlic and sauté for about 1 minute.
3. Add ground turkey and cook for about 7-8 minutes, breaking up the chunks with a wooden spoon.
4. Add tomatoes and chili powder and cook for about 4 more minutes.
5. Add the potatoes and broth and bring to a boil.
6. Adjust the heat to low and cook, covered for about 20-25 minutes, stirring occasionally.
7. Stir in salt and black pepper and serve hot.

Meatballs & Spinach Soup

Servings|6   Time|45 minutes
Nutritional Content (per serving):
Cal| 203   Fat| 10.8g   Protein| 23.1g   Carbs| 3.7g   Fiber| 1g

Ingredients:

For Meatballs:

- ❖ Extra-Lean ground turkey (1 pound)
- ❖ Garlic clove (1, minced)
- ❖ Egg (1, beaten)
- ❖ Parmesan cheese (¼ cup, grated)
- ❖ Salt and ground black pepper, as required

For Soup:

- ❖ Olive oil (1 tablespoon)
- ❖ Small onion (1, finely chopped)
- ❖ Garlic clove (1, minced)
- ❖ Chicken broth (6 cups)
- ❖ Fresh spinach (7 cups, chopped)
- ❖ Salt and ground black pepper, as required

Directions:

1. For meatballs: in a bowl, add all ingredients and mix until well combined.
2. Make equal-sized small balls from mixture.
3. In a large soup saucepan, heat oil over medium heat and sauté onion for about 5-6 minutes.
4. Add the garlic and sauté for about 1 minute.
5. Add the broth and bring to a boil.
6. Carefully place the balls in saucepan and bring to a boil.
7. Now adjust the heat to low and cook for about 10 minutes.
8. Stir in the kale and bring the soup to a gentle simmer.
9. Simmer for about 2-3 minutes.
10. Season with salt and black pepper and serve hot.

Beef & Lentil Soup

Servings|8 Time|2¼ hours
Nutritional Content (per serving):
Cal| 367   Fat| 7.7g   Protein| 31.1g   Carbs| 43.1g   Fiber| 9.5g

Ingredients:

- Olive oil (2 tablespoons)
- Salt and ground black pepper, as required
- Large celery stalk (1, chopped)
- Large onion (1, chopped)
- Dried rosemary (1 teaspoon)
- Large sweet potato (1, peeled and chopped)
- Red lentils (2 cups, rinsed)
- Beef chuck (1 pound, trimmed and cut into 1-inch cubes)
- Large carrot (1, peeled and chopped)
- Garlic cloves (6, chopped)
- Dried oregano (1 teaspoon)
- Chicken broth (8-9 cups)
- Tomatoes (4-5 cups, chopped)
- Fresh parsley (¼ cup, chopped)

Directions:

1. Season the beef cubes with salt and black pepper evenly.
2. In a large soup saucepan, heat the olive oil over medium-high heat and cook the beef cubes for about 8 minutes or until browned from all sides.
3. With a slotted spoon, transfer the beef into a bowl and set aside.
4. In the same saucepan, add the carrot, celery onion, garlic and dried herbs over medium heat and cook for about 5 minutes.
5. Add sweet potato and cook for about 4-5 minutes.
6. Add cooked beef, tomatoes and broth and bring to a boil over high heat.
7. Adjust the heat to low and cook, covered for about 1 hour.
8. Add the lentils and cook, covered for about 40 minutes.
9. Stir in black pepper and remove from the heat.
10. Serve hot with the garnishing of parsley.

Salmon, Quinoa & Spinach Soup

Servings|8   Time|1 hour 25 minutes
Nutritional Content (per serving):
Cal| 302   Fat| 14.4g   Protein| 23.7g   Carbs| 20.9g   Fiber| 3.7g

Ingredients:

- Onions (2 cups, chopped)
- Garlic cloves (2, chopped)
- Fresh mushrooms (1 cup, sliced)
- Chicken broth (8 cups)
- Fresh baby spinach (6 cups)
- Fresh cilantro (1 cup, chopped)
- Salt and ground black pepper, as required
- Celery stalk (1 cup, chopped)
- Fresh ginger (2 tablespoons, chopped finely)
- Quinoa (1 cup, rinsed)
- Salmon fillets (20 ounces, cut into large chunks)
- Unsweetened coconut milk (1 cup)

Directions:

1. In a large soup saucepan, add onions, celery stalk, garlic, ginger root, mushrooms, quinoa and broth and bring to a boil.
2. Now adjust the heat to low and simmer, covered for about 45 minutes.
3. Arrange the salmon chunks over the soup mixture.
4. Simmer, covered for about 15 minutes.
5. Stir in remaining ingredients and simmer for about 5 minutes.
6. Serve hot.

Lentil & Sweet Potato Soup

Servings|6   Time|55 minutes
Nutritional Content (per serving):
Cal| 239   Fat| 4.2g   Protein| 12.4g   Carbs| 38.9g   Fiber| 9.3g

Ingredients:

- Vegetable oil (1 tablespoon)
- Tomatoes (1¾ cups, chopped)
- Brown lentils (½ cup, rinsed)
- Fresh kale (4 cups, tough ribs removed and chopped)
- Salt and ground black pepper, as required
- Leeks (4, chopped)
- Vegetable broth (6 cups)
- Sweet potatoes (2, peeled and cubed)
- Fresh thyme (1 tablespoon , chopped)

Directions:

1. In a large-sized soup saucepan, heat oil over medium heat and sauté leeks for about 3-4 minutes.
2. Add tomatoes and cook for 5-6 minutes, crushing with the back of a spoon.
3. Add broth and bring to a boil.
4. Add lentils, sweet potato, kale, and thyme and again, bring to a boil.
5. Now adjust the heat to low and simmer, covered for about 25-30 minutes or until desired doneness.
6. Stir in salt and black pepper and serve hot.

Chicken & Swiss Chard Stew

Servings|4   Time|50 minutes
Nutritional Content (per serving):
Cal| 494   Fat| 1.36.6g   Protein| 30g   Carbs| 17.6g   Fiber| 5.8g

Ingredients:

- Extra-virgin olive oil (2 tablespoons)
- Fresh ginger (1 tablespoon, minced
- Ground coriander (1 teaspoon)
- Boneless, skinless chicken thighs 3 (6-ounce), cut into 1-inch pieces)
- Salt and ground black pepper, as required
- Fresh lemon juice (2 tablespoons)
- Yellow onion 1, chopped
- Garlic (1 tablespoon), minced
- Ground turmeric (1 teaspoon)
- Ground cumin (1 teaspoon)
- Paprika (1 teaspoon)
- Tomatoes 4, chopped)
- Unsweetened coconut milk (14 ounces)
- Fresh Swiss chard (6 cups, chopped)

Directions:

1. Heat oil in a large heavy-bottomed saucepan over medium heat and sauté the onion for about 3-4 minutes.
2. Add the ginger, garlic, and spices, and sauté for about 1 minute.
3. Add the chicken and cook for about 4-5 minutes.
4. Add the tomatoes, coconut milk, salt, and black pepper, and bring to a gentle simmer.
5. Now, adjust the heat to low and simmer, covered for about 10-15 minutes.
6. Stir in the Swiss chard and cook for about 4-5 minutes.
7. Add in lemon juice and remove from the heat.
8. Serve hot.

Beef & Pumpkin Stew

Servings|4   Time|2 hours 20 minutes
Nutritional Content (per serving):
Cal| 355   Fat| 14.7g   Protein| 2.4g   Carbs| 90.6g   Fiber| 37.5g

Ingredients:

- Beef stew meat (1 pound, trimmed and cubed)
- Extra-virgin olive oil (2 tablespoons, divided)
- Celery stalks (2, chopped)
- Pumpkin (2 cups, peeled and cubed)
- Fresh cilantro (¼ cup, chopped)
- Salt and ground black pepper, as required
- Medium carrot (1, peeled and chopped finely)
- Medium onion (1, chopped)
- Tomatoes (3 cups, chopped finely)
- Water (3-4 cups)

Directions:

1. Season the beef with salt and black pepper evenly.
2. In a large saucepan, heat 1 tablespoon of oil over medium heat and sear beef for about 4-5 minutes.
3. Transfer the beef into a large bowl and set aside.
4. In the same saucepan, heat the remaining oil over medium heat and sauté carrot, celery and onion for about 5 minutes.
5. Add pumpkin and tomatoes and sauté for about 5 minutes.
6. Add water and beef and bring to a boil over high heat.
7. Now adjust the heat to low and simmer, covered for about 1 hour.
8. Uncover and simmer for about 50 minutes.
9. Serve hot with the garnishing of cilantro.

Pork & Beans Stew

Servings|8   Time|3 hours 35 minutes
Nutritional Content (per serving):
Cal| 456   Fat| 23.8g   Protein| 35.4g   Carbs| 43.2g   Fiber| 23.2g

Ingredients:

- Dried Great Northern beans (1 pound, rinsed)
- Tomatoes (2½ cups, chopped)
- Pork shoulder (2 pounds, cut into 1-inch chunks)
- Fresh thyme (2 tablespoons, chopped)
- Ground allspice (1 teaspoon)
- Chicken broth (3½ cups)
- Onion (1, chopped)
- Carrots (3, peeled and cut into ½-inch pieces)
- Fresh parsley (2 tablespoons, chopped)
- Salt and ground black pepper, as required

Directions:

1. Preheat your oven to 250 degrees F.
2. In a large saucepan of water, add the beans and cook for about 20 minutes.
3. Remove from the heat and drain the beans.
4. In a large casserole dish, place the beans and remaining ingredients and stir to combine.
5. Cover the casserole dish and bake for approximately 3 hours.
6. Serve hot.

Black Beans & Pumpkin Stew

Servings|6   Time|50 minutes
Nutritional Content (per serving):
Cal| 290   Fat| 6.5g   Protein| 16.3g   Carbs| 44.7g   Fiber| 15.6g

Ingredients:

- Olive oil (2 tablespoons)
- Garlic cloves (4, minced)
- Red chili powder (1 teaspoon)
- Black beans (2 (15-ounce) cans, rinsed and drained)
- Tomatoes (1 cup, chopped finely)
- Fresh cilantro (¼ cup, chopped)
- Medium onion (1, chopped)
- Ground cumin (1 tablespoon)
- Salt and ground black pepper, as required
- Sugar-free pumpkin puree (1 (16-ounce) can)
- Chicken broth (2 cups)
- Chicken broth (2 cups)

Directions:

1. In a large soup saucepan, heat the oil over medium heat and sauté the onion for about 4-5 minutes.
2. Add the garlic, cumin, chili powder and black pepper and sauté for about 1 minute.
3. Add the black beans, pumpkin, tomatoes and broth and stir to combine.
4. Increase the heat to medium-high and bring to a boil.
5. Now adjust the heat and simmer uncovered for about 25 minutes, stirring occasionally.
6. Remove from the heat and stir in yogurt.
7. With an immersion blender, blend the soup until smooth.
8. Serve hot with the garnishing of cilantro.

Chickpeas & Kale Stew

Servings|4   Time|50 minutes
Nutritional Content (per serving):
Cal| 300   Fat| 9.5g   Protein| 11.6g   Carbs| 44.8g   Fiber| 9.2g

Ingredients:

- Extra-virgin olive oil (2 tablespoons)
- Large tomatoes (2, chopped finely)
- Vegetable broth (2 cups)
- Fresh kale (3 cups, tough ribs removed and chopped)
- Fresh lemon juice (1 tablespoon)
- Medium onion (1, chopped)
- Carrots (2 cups, peeled
- Ground cumin (1 teaspoon)
- Red pepper flakes (½ teaspoon, crushed)
- Cooked chickpeas (2 cups)
- Salt and ground black pepper, as required

Directions:

1. Heat olive oil in a large soup saucepan over medium heat and sauté the onion and carrot for about 6-8 minutes.
2. Add the tomatoes, cumin and red pepper flakes and cook for about 2-3 minutes.
3. Add the broth and bring to a boil.
4. Adjust the heat to low and simmer for about 10 minutes.
5. Stir in the chickpeas and simmer for about 5 minutes.
6. Stir in the kale and simmer for 4-5 minutes more.
7. Stir in the lemon juice, salt and black pepper and serve hot.

Lentils & Quinoa Stew

Servings|6   Time|48 minutes
Nutritional Content (per serving):
Cal| 253   Fat| 4g   Protein| 12.4g   Carbs| 43.6g   Fiber| 13.9g

Ingredients:

- Extra-virgin olive oil (1 tablespoon)
- Onion (1, chopped)
- Tomatoes (4 cups, chopped)
- Quinoa (½ cup, rinsed)
- Red chili powder (1 teaspoon)
- Fresh spinach (2 cups, chopped)
- Carrots (3, peeled and chopped)
- Celery stalks (3, chopped)
- Garlic cloves (4, minced)
- Red lentils (1 cup, rinsed)
- Ground cumin (1½ teaspoons)
- Vegetable broth (4-5 cups)

Directions:

1. In a large saucepan, heat the oil over medium heat and cook the celery, onion and carrot for about 8 minutes, stirring frequently.
2. Add the garlic and sauté for about 1 minute.
3. Add the remaining ingredients except for spinach and bring to a boil.
4. Now adjust the heat to low and simmer, covered for about 20 minutes.
5. Stir in spinach and simmer for about 3-4 minutes.
6. Serve hot.

Lentil & Barley Stew

Servings|8   Time|1 hour 5 minutes
Nutritional Content (per serving):
Cal| 265   Fat| 6g   Protein| 15.3g   Carbs| 38.7g   Fiber| 13.2g

Ingredients:

- Olive oil (2 tablespoons)
- Large onion (1, chopped)
- Garlic cloves (2, minced)
- Ground cumin (1 teaspoon)
- Barley (1 cup)
- Tomatoes (2½ cups, chopped finely)
- Fresh spinach (4 cups, torn)
- Carrots (2, peeled and chopped)
- Celery stalks (2, chopped)
- Ground coriander (1 teaspoon)
- Cayenne pepper (1 teaspoon)
- Red lentils (1 cup, rinsed)
- Vegetable broth (8 cups)
- Salt and ground black pepper, as required

Directions:

1. In a large saucepan, heat oil over medium heat and sauté carrots, onion and celery for about 5 minutes.
2. Add garlic and spices and sauté for about 1 minute.
3. Add barley, lentils, tomatoes and broth and bring to a boil.
4. Now adjust the heat to low and simmer, covered for about 40 minutes.
5. Stir in spinach, salt and black pepper and simmer for about 3-4 minutes.
6. Serve hot.

Quinoa & Veggie Stew

Servings|4   Time|1¼ hours
Nutritional Content (per serving):
Cal| 237   Fat| 8.6g   Protein| 6.9g   Carbs| 36.2g   Fiber| 6g

Ingredients:

- ❖ Olive oil (2 tablespoons)
- ❖ Salt, as required
- ❖ Garlic cloves (3, minced)
- ❖ Ground cumin (1 teaspoon)
- ❖ Tomatoes (2½ cups, chopped finely)
- ❖ Fresh kale (3 cups, tough ribs removed and chopped)

- ❖ Large onion (1, chopped)
- ❖ Sweet potatoes (2 cups, peeled and cubed)
- ❖ Cayenne pepper (1 teaspoon)
- ❖ Dry quinoa (½ cup, rinsed)
- ❖ Water (3 cups)
- ❖ Fresh lime juice (1 tablespoon)

Directions:

1. In a soup saucepan, heat the grapeseed oil over medium heat and cook the onion with a few pinches of salt for about 4-5 minutes, stirring occasionally.
2. Add the butternut squash and cook for about 3-4 minutes.
3. Stir in the garlic and spices and cook for about 1 minute.
4. Stir in the tomatoes, quinoa and water and bring to a boil.
5. Now, adjust the heat to low and simmer, covered for about 35 minutes.
6. Stir in the kale and cook for about 10 minutes.
7. Stir in lime juice and serve hot.

Sweet Potato & Kale Stew

Servings|6   Time|55 minutes
Nutritional Content (per serving):
Cal| 280   Fat| 17.2g   Protein| 13.4g   Carbs| 22g   Fiber| 4.3g

Ingredients:

- Olive oil (2 tablespoons)
- Medium sweet potato (1, peeled and cubed into ½-inch size)
- Garlic cloves (4, minced)
- Red pepper flakes (¼ teaspoon, crushed)
- Tomato paste (1 (6-ounce) can)
- Fresh kale (3 cups, tough ribs removed and chopped)
- Medium onion (1, chopped)
- Fresh ginger (1 teaspoon, minced)
- Serrano pepper (1, chopped)
- Ground cumin (1 teaspoon)
- Natural peanut butter (½ cup)
- Vegetable broth (6 cups)
- Salt and ground black pepper, as required

Directions:

1. In a Dutch oven, heat oil over medium heat and sauté for onion for about 4-6 minutes.
2. Add sweet potato and cook for about 5-8 minutes.
3. Add ginger, garlic, serrano pepper and spices and sauté for about 1 minute.
4. Add peanut butter and tomato paste and cook for about 2 minutes.
5. Add broth and bring to a boil.
6. Cover and cook for about 5 minutes.
7. Stir in kale and adjust the heat to low.
8. Simmer for about 15 minutes.
9. Remove from heat and set aside to cool slightly.
10. With a potato masher, blend half of sweet potatoes.
11. Return the saucepan over medium heat and simmer for about 2-3 minutes.
12. Season with salt and black pepper and serve hot.

Turkey & Beans Chili

Servings|6   Time|1 hour
Nutritional Content (per serving):
Cal| 270   Fat| 10.9g   Protein| 21.3g   Carbs| 27g   Fiber| 6.9g

Ingredients:

- Olive oil (2 tablespoons)
- Onion (1, chopped)
- Garlic cloves (2, chopped)
- Water (2 cups)
- Ground cumin (1 teaspoon)
- Ground cinnamon (½ teaspoon)
- Scallion greens (¼ cup, chopped)
- Bell pepper (1, seeded and chopped)
- Lean ground turkey (1 pound)
- Tomatoes (3 cups, chopped finely)
- Red kidney beans (1 (15-ounce) can, rinsed and drained)
- Frozen corn (1½ cups, thawed)

Directions:

1. In a large Dutch oven, heat the olive oil over medium-low heat and sauté bell pepper, onion and garlic for about 5 minutes.
2. Add turkey and cook for about 5-6 minutes, breaking up the chunks with a wooden spoon.
3. Add water, tomatoes and spices and bring to a boil over high heat.
4. Adjust the heat to medium-low and stir in beans and corn.
5. Simmer, covered for about 30 minutes, stirring occasionally.
6. Serve hot with the topping of scallion greens.

Beef & Beans Chili

Servings|10 Time|1 hour 5 minutes
Nutritional Content (per serving):
Cal| 407   Fat| 8.5g   Protein| 41.3g   Carbs| 42.4g   Fiber| 14.4g

Ingredients:

- Lean ground beef (2 pounds)
- Bell pepper (2½ cups, seeded and chopped)
- Serrano pepper (1, chopped)
- Dried thyme (½ tablespoon)
- Paprika (1 tablespoon)
- Ground cumin (1 tablespoon)
- Tomatoes (4 cups, chopped)
- Balsamic vinegar (2 tablespoons)
- Olive oil (1 tablespoon)
- Onion (1½ cups, chopped)
- Garlic cloves (2, minced)
- Dried oregano ½ tablespoon)
- Red chili powder (2 tablespoons)
- Black beans (3 (15-ounce) cans, rinsed and drained)
- Water, as required
- Tomato paste (8 ounces)

Directions:

1. Heat a Dutch oven over medium heat and cook beef for about 5-7 minutes or until browned completely.
2. With a slotted spoon, transfer the beef into a bowl.
3. Drain the grease from the saucepan.
4. In the same saucepan, heat oil over medium-high heat and sauté the bell pepper and onion for about 5-6 minutes.
5. Add garlic, Serrano pepper, oregano, thyme and spices and sauté for about 1 minute.
6. Stir in cooked beef, beans, tomatoes and enough water to cover and bring to a boil.
7. Stir in tomato paste and again bring to a boil.
8. Now adjust the heat to low and simmer, covered for about 30-35 minutes.
9. Remove the saucepan of chili from the heat and immediately stir in vinegar.
10. Serve hot.

Beans & Sweet Potato Chili

Servings|4   Time|2½ hours
Nutritional Content (per serving):
Cal| 373   Fat| 9.9g   Protein| 17.1g   Carbs| 59.6g   Fiber| 16.5g

Ingredients:

- Olive oil (2 tablespoons)
- Small bell peppers (2, seeded and chopped)
- Cayenne pepper (1 teaspoon)
- Medium sweet potato (1, peeled and chopped)
- Canned red kidney beans (3 cups, rinsed and drained)
- Vegetable broth (2 cups)
- Onion (1, chopped)
- Garlic cloves (4, minced)
- Ground cumin (1 teaspoon)
- Red chili powder (1 tablespoon)
- Tomatoes (3 cups, chopped finely)
- Canned corn kernels (1 cup)
- Salt and ground black pepper, as required

Directions:

1. In a large saucepan, heat oil over medium-high heat and sauté onion and bell peppers for about 3-4 minutes.
2. Add garlic and spices and sauté for 1 minute.
3. Add sweet potato and cook for about 4-5 minutes.
4. Add remaining all ingredients and bring to a boil.
5. Now adjust the heat to medium-low and simmer, covered for about 1-2 hours.
6. Season with salt and black pepper and serve hot.

Chickpeas & Zucchini Chili

Servings|8   Time|1 hour 25 minutes
Nutritional Content (per serving):
Cal| 147   Fat| 1.9g   Protein| 6.2g   Carbs| 28.2g   Fiber| 6.2g

Ingredients:

- Olive oil (2 tablespoons)
- Large bell pepper (1, seeded and chopped)
- Cayenne pepper (1 tablespoon)
- Medium zucchinis (2, chopped)
- Cooked chickpeas (3 cups)
- Medium onion (1, chopped)
- Garlic cloves (4, minced)
- Dried thyme (1 teaspoon)
- Salt, as required
- Tomatoes (3 cups, chopped)
- Water (2 cups)

Directions:

1. In a saucepan, heat the avocado oil over medium heat and sauté the onion and bell pepper for about 8 to 9 minutes.
2. Add the garlic, thyme, cayenne pepper and salt and sauté for about 1 minute.
3. Add in all remaining ingredients and cook until boiling.
4. Now, adjust the heat to low and simmer for about 1 hour or until desired thickness.
5. Serve hot.

Stuffed Chicken Breast

Servings|4   Time|40 minutes
Nutritional Content (per serving):
Cal| 223   Fat| 8.7g   Protein| 32.3g   Carbs| 3.6g   Fiber| 0.9g

Ingredients:

- Olive oil (1 tablespoon)
- Pepperoni pepper (1, seeded and sliced thinly)
- Garlic (3 teaspoons, minced)
- Skinless, boneless chicken breasts (4 (5-ounce), butterflied and pounded)
- Small onion (1, chopped)
- Bell pepper (½, seeded and sliced thinly)
- Fresh spinach (1 cup, chopped)
- Dried oregano (½ teaspoon)
- Salt and ground black pepper, as required

Directions:

1. Preheat your oven to 350 degrees F. Line a baking sheet with parchment paper.
2. In a saucepan, heat the olive oil over medium heat and sauté onion and both peppers for about 1 minute.
3. Add the garlic and spinach and cook for about 2-3 minutes or until just wilted.
4. Stir in oregano, salt and black pepper and remove the saucepan from heat.
5. Place the chicken mixture into the middle of each butterflied chicken breast.
6. Fold each chicken breast over filling to make a little pocket and secure with toothpicks.
7. Arrange the chicken breasts onto the prepared baking sheet.
8. Bake for approximately 18-20 minutes.
9. Serve hot.

Chicken & Veggies Bake

Servings|6   Time|55 minutes
Nutritional Content (per serving):
Cal| 288   Fat| 16.8g   Protein| 22.6g   Carbs| 13.9g   Fiber| 3.6g

Ingredients:

- Broccoli florets (1 pound)
- Olive oil (1 tablespoon)
- Small onion (1, chopped)
- Boneless, skinless chicken breasts (2 cups, cubed)
- Plain Greek yogurt (1 (5.3-ounce) container)
- Salt and ground black pepper, as required
- Water (¼ cup)
- Fresh mushrooms (1 pound, sliced)
- Almond flour (3 tablespoons)
- Unsweetened almond milk (1½ cups)
- Mayonnaise (¼ cup)
- Mexican cheese (¾ cup, shredded)

Directions:

1. Preheat your oven to 350 degrees F. Grease a casserole dish.
2. In a microwave-safe bowl, place the broccoli and water and microwave on high for about 3-4 minutes.
3. Remove from microwave and drain the broccoli completely. Set aside.
4. Heat olive oil in a wok over medium-high heat and cook the mushrooms and onion for about 5-6 minutes, stirring frequently.
5. Add the chicken and cook for about 2-3 minutes.
6. Drain any liquid from the saucepan.
7. Sprinkle flour over chicken mixture and cook for about 3-4 minutes, stirring continuously.
8. Stir in cooked broccoli and cook for about 1 minute.
9. Add the yogurt, mayonnaise, salt and black pepper and gently stir to combine.
10. Remove the saucepan of chicken mixture from heat and transfer into the prepared casserole dish.
11. With a spoon, spread the chicken mixture evenly and sprinkle with Mexican cheese.
12. Bake for approximately 20 minutes or until cheese is bubbly.

Chicken & Sweet Potato Curry

Servings|4   Time|30 minutes
Nutritional Content (per serving):
Cal| 325   Fat| 13.1g   Protein| 27.4g   Carbs| 24.2g   Fiber| 4g

Ingredients:

- ❖ Skinless, boneless chicken breast (1 pound, cut into chunks)
- ❖ Onion (½, chopped)
- ❖ Garlic cloves (2, minced)
- ❖ Curry powder (1 teaspoon)
- ❖ Chicken broth (½ cup)
- ❖ Unsweetened coconut milk (14 ounces)
- ❖ Salt and ground black pepper, as required
- ❖ Olive oil (2 tablespoons, divided)
- ❖ Fresh ginger (1 teaspoon, minced)
- ❖ Large sweet potatoes (2, peeled and cubed)

Directions:

1. Sprinkle the chicken chunks with salt and black pepper.
2. In a large wok, heat 1 tablespoon of oil over medium heat and stir fry the chicken chunks for about 3-4 minutes per side.
3. Transfer the chicken chunks onto a plate.
4. In the same wok, heat the remaining oil over medium heat and sauté onion for about 5-7 minutes.
5. Add garlic, ginger and curry powder and sauté for about 1-2 minutes.
6. Add chicken and remaining ingredients and stir to combine well.
7. Cover the saucepan and simmer for about 15-20 minutes.
8. Stir in salt and black pepper and serve hot.

Chicken & Green Beans Curry

Servings|4   Time|45 minutes
Nutritional Content (per serving):
Cal| 385   Fat| 26.7g   Protein| 29.5g   Carbs| 9g   Fiber| 3g

Ingredients:

- Skinless, boneless chicken breasts (1 pound, cubed)
- Unsweetened coconut milk (1 cup)
- Fresh green beans (2 cups, trimmed)
- Fresh basil (¼ cup, chopped)
- Olive oil (1 tablespoon)
- Green curry paste (2 tablespoons)
- Chicken broth (1 cup)
- Salt and ground black pepper, as required

Directions:

1. In a wok, heat oil over medium heat and sauté the curry paste for about 1-2 minutes.
2. Add the chicken and cook for about 8-10 minutes.
3. Add coconut milk and broth and bring to a boil.
4. Now adjust the heat low and cook for about 8-10 minutes.
5. Add asparagus, green beans, salt and black pepper and cook for about 4-5 minutes or until desired doneness.
6. Serve hot.

Chicken, Rice & Beans Casserole

Servings|8   Time|1 hour 40 minutes
Nutritional Content (per serving):
Cal| 475   Fat| 12.9g   Protein| 37.8g   Carbs| 54.2g   Fiber| 13.1g

Ingredients:

- Brown rice (1/3 cup, rinsed)
- Olive oil (1 tablespoon)
- Cooked chicken breast (1 (6 ounces), cut into small pieces)
- Fresh mushrooms (½ cup, sliced)
- Black beans (1 (15-ounce) can, rinsed and drained)
- Swiss cheese (2 cups, shredded)
- Vegetable broth (1 cup)
- Onion (1/3 cup, chopped)
- Medium zucchini (1, sliced thinly)
- Ground cumin (½ teaspoon)
- Cayenne pepper (¼ teaspoon)
- Carrots (1/3 cup, peeled and shredded)

Directions:

1. In a saucepan, add the rice and broth over medium-high heat and bring to a rolling boil.
2. Now adjust the heat to low and simmer, covered for about 45 minutes or until rice is tender.
3. Preheat your oven to 350 degrees F. Lightly grease a large casserole dish.
4. Meanwhile, in a wok, heat olive oil over medium heat and sauté the onion for about 4-5 minutes.
5. Stir in the chicken, zucchini, mushrooms, cumin and cayenne pepper and cook for about 4-5 minutes.
6. In a large bowl, add the cooked rice, chicken mixture, black beans, carrots, green chilies and 1 cup of Swiss cheese and mix well.
7. Transfer the chicken mixture into the prepared casserole dish evenly and sprinkle with the remaining Swiss cheese.
8. With a piece of foil, cover the casserole dish loosely and bake for approximately 30 minutes.
9. Uncover the casserole dish and bake for approximately 10 minutes.
10. Remove from the oven and set aside for about 5 minutes before serving.

Ground Turkey with Veggies

Servings|2 Time|10 minutes
Nutritional Content (per serving):
Cal| 328   Fat| 19.4g   Protein| 37.9g   Carbs| 6.3g   Fiber| 1.9g

Ingredients:

- ❖ Lean ground turkey (1¾ pounds)
- ❖ Medium onion (1, chopped)
- ❖ Garlic cloves (6, minced)
- ❖ Fresh green beans (2 cups, trimmed and cut into 1-inch pieces)
- ❖ Salt and ground black pepper, as required
- ❖ Olive oil (2 tablespoons)
- ❖ Carrot (1 cup, peeled and chopped)
- ❖ Chicken broth (¼ cup)
- ❖ Red pepper flakes (¼ teaspoon, crushed)

Directions:

1. Heat a non-stick wok over medium-high heat and cook the turkey for about 6-8 minutes or until browned.
2. With a slotted spoon, transfer the turkey into a bowl and discard the grease from wok.
3. In the same wok, heat oil over medium heat and sauté onion, carrot and garlic for about 5 minutes
4. Add asparagus and cooked turkey and stir to combine.
5. Add the broth, red pepper flakes, salt and black pepper and bring to a boil.
6. Now adjust the heat to medium-low and cook for about 6-8 minutes, stirring frequently.
7. Serve hot.

Beef & Raisins Curry

Servings|4   Time|1 hour 35 minutes
Nutritional Content (per serving):
Cal| 269   Fat| 33.8g   Protein| 57.6g   Carbs| 22.3g   Fiber| 2.7g

Ingredients:

- Olive oil (3 tablespoons)
- Medium onions (2, sliced into ¼-inch thick rounds)
- Garlic cloves (3, crushed)
- Ground turmeric (1 teaspoon)
- Salt, as required
- Beef broth (2½ cups)
- Golden raisins (½ cup)
- Chuck roast (1½ pounds, trimmed and cut into 1½-inch cubes)
- Red chili powder (1 teaspoon)
- Garam masala powder (1 teaspoon)
- Unsweetened desiccated coconut (¼ cup)

Directions:

1. In a Dutch oven, melt 2 tablespoons of the butter over medium heat and cook the beef cubes in 2 batches for about 3 minutes.
2. With a slotted spoon, transfer the beef cubes onto a plate.
3. In the saucepan, melt the remaining butter over medium heat and cook the onions for about 10 minutes, stirring frequently.
4. Add the garlic and cook for about 1 minute.
5. Stir in the cooked beef chili powder, turmeric, garam masala and salt and cook for about 1 minute, stirring continuously.
6. Stir in the broth, raisins and coconut and bring to a gentle boil.
7. Now adjust the heat to low and cook, covered for about 45-60 minutes.
8. Serve hot.

Stuffed Steak

Servings|6   Time|55 minutes
Nutritional Content (per serving):
Cal| 264   Fat| 11.9g   Protein| 32.8g   Carbs| 5.3g   Fiber| 0.9g

Ingredients:

- Flank steak (1½ pounds, trimmed)
- Extra-virgin olive oil (1 tablespoon)
- Medium bell pepper (1, seeded and chopped)
- Salt and ground black pepper, as required
- Small garlic cloves (2, minced)
- Fresh kale (6 ounces, tough ribs removed and chopped finely)
- Tomato (1, chopped finely)

Directions:

1. Preheat your oven to 425 degrees F. Grease a large baking dish.
2. Place the flank steak onto a clean cutting board.
3. Hold a sharp knife parallel to the work surface, slice the steak horizontally, without cutting all the way through, that you can open like a book.
4. With a pounder, flatten the steak to an even thickness.
5. Sprinkle the steak with a little salt and black pepper evenly.
6. In a wok, heat the oil over medium heat and sauté the garlic for about 1 minute.
7. Add the kale and cook for about 3 minutes.
8. Stir in the bell pepper and tomato and immediately remove from heat.
9. Transfer the spinach mixture into a bowl and set aside to cool slightly
10. Place the filling on top of steak evenly.
11. Roll up the steak to seal the filling.
12. With cotton twine, tie the steak.
13. Place the steak roll into the prepared baking dish.
14. Bake for approximately 30-35 minutes.
15. Remove from the oven and let it cool slightly before slicing.
16. Cut the roll into desired-sized slices and serve.

Steak with Cashews

Servings|5   Time|35 minutes
Nutritional Content (per serving):
Cal| 422   Fat| 22.8g   Protein| 34.1g   Carbs| 21.8g   Fiber| 0.9g

Ingredients:

- Arrowroot flour (2 tablespoons)
- Flank steak (1½ pounds, cut into ¼-inch thick slices)
- Onion (1, sliced)
- Fresh ginger (1 teaspoon, minced)
- Maple syrup (1/3 cup)
- Low-sodium soy sauce (½ cup)
- Cashews (5 tablespoons)
- Salt and ground black pepper, as required
- Olive oil (¼ cup, divided)
- Garlic cloves (2, minced)
- Red pepper flakes (¼ teaspoon, crushed)
- Beef broth (½ cup)
- Fresh parsley (2 tablespoons, chopped)

Directions:

1. In a bowl, mix together arrowroot flour, salt and black pepper.
2. Coat the beef slices in the arrowroot flour mixture evenly. Set aside for about 10-15 minutes.
3. For sauce: in a saucepan, heat 1 tablespoon of oil over medium heat and sauté the onion for about 3-4 minutes.
4. Add garlic, ginger and red pepper flakes and sauté for about 1 minute.
5. Add the maple syrup, broth and soy sauce and stir to combine well.
6. Adjust the heat to high and cook for about 3 minutes, stirring continuously.
7. Remove the sauce from heat and set aside.
8. In a large wok, heat remaining oil over medium-high heat and fry the beef slices for about 3-4 minutes.
9. With a slotted spoon, transfer the beef onto a paper towel-lined plate to drain.
10. Remove the oil from wok, leaving about 1 tablespoon inside.
11. Return the beef slices into wok over medium heat and sear the beef slices for about 2-3 minutes.
12. Stir in sauce and cook for about 3-5 minutes.
13. Serve hot with the garnishing of cashews and parsley.

Ground Beef with Veggies

Servings|2   Time|10 minutes
Nutritional Content (per serving):
Cal| 293   Fat| 14.4g   Protein| 36.6g   Carbs| 3.6g   Fiber| 1g

Ingredients:

- ❖ Lean ground beef (1 pound)
- ❖ Garlic cloves (2, minced)
- ❖ Fresh mushrooms (2 cups, sliced)
- ❖ Beef broth (1/3 cup)
- ❖ Olive oil (2 tablespoons)
- ❖ Onion (½, chopped)
- ❖ Fresh spinach (2 cups, torn)
- ❖ Salt and ground black pepper, as required

Directions:

1. Heat a large non-stick wok over medium-high heat and cook the ground beef for about 8-10 minutes, breaking up the chunks with a wooden spoon.
2. With a slotted spoon, transfer the beef into a bowl.
3. In the same wok, add the onion and garlic for about 3 minutes.
4. Add the mushrooms and cook for about 5-7 minutes.
5. Add the cooked beef, spinach and broth and bring to a boil.
6. Adjust the heat to medium-low and simmer for about 3 minutes.
7. Serve hot.

Stuffed Leg of Lamb

Servings|14   Time|2 hours 25 minutes
Nutritional Content (per serving):
Cal| 340   Fat| 15.3g   Protein| 46.6g   Carbs| 1.2g   Fiber| 0.3g

Ingredients:

- Olive oil (4 teaspoons, divided)
- Garlic cloves (2, chopped finely)
- Sun-dried tomatoes in olive oil (2 tablespoons, drained and chopped
- Boneless leg of lamb (1 (4-5-pound), trimmed and butterflied)
- Scallions (¼ cup, chopped)
- Fresh spinach (1 cup, shredded)
- Fresh basil leaves (¼ cup, shredded)
- Pine nuts (2 tablespoons)
- Lemon pepper (3 teaspoons, divided)
- Feta cheese (½ cup, crumbled)

Directions:

1. Preheat your oven to 325 degrees F. Arrange a greased rack into a roasting saucepan.
2. In a medium wok, heat 3 teaspoons of olive oil over medium heat and sauté the scallion and garlic for about 2 minutes.
3. Stir in the spinach, sun-dried tomatoes, basil, pine nuts, and 1 teaspoon of lemon pepper and cook for about 2-3 minutes, stirring frequently.
4. Remove from the heat and stir in feta cheese. Set aside.
5. Remove the strings from leg of lamb and open it.
6. Place the stuffing in the center of meat evenly and roll to seal the filling.
7. Carefully tie the leg of lamb with kitchen string.
8. Coat the rolled leg of lamb with the remaining oil and sprinkle with 1 teaspoon of lemon pepper.
9. Arrange the rolled leg of lamb into the prepared roasting saucepan.
10. Roast for about 2 hours.
11. Remove the leg of lamb from the oven and place onto a cutting board.
12. With a piece of foil, cover the leg of lamb for 10 minutes before slicing.
13. Cut into desired-sized slices and serve.

Lamb with Spinach

Servings|6   Time|3¼ hours
Nutritional Content (per serving):
Cal| 471   Fat| 32.5g   Protein| 33.6g   Carbs| 13.2g   Fiber| 4.7g

Ingredients:

- Olive oil (2 tablespoons)
- Salt, as required
- Medium onions (2, chopped)
- Fresh ginger (3 tablespoons, minced)
- Ground cumin (1 tablespoon)
- Ground turmeric (1 tablespoon)
- Tomatoes (¼ cup, chopped)
- Frozen spinach (30 ounces, thawed and squeezed)
- Ground black pepper, as required
- Lamb necks (2 pounds, trimmed and cut into 2-inch pieces crosswise)
- Garlic cloves (4, minced)
- Ground coriander (2 tablespoons)
- Plain Greek yogurt (¼ cup)
- Boiling water (2 cups)
- Fresh lemon juice (1 tablespoon)
- Garam masala powder (1½ tablespoons)

Directions:

1. Preheat your oven to 300 degrees F.
2. In a large Dutch oven, heat the oil over medium-high heat and stir fry the lamb necks with a little salt for about 4-5 minutes.
3. With a slotted spoon, transfer the lamb onto a plate.
4. In the same saucepan, add onion over medium heat and sauté for about 10 minutes.
5. Add the ginger, garlic and spices and sauté for about 1 minute.
6. Add the yogurt and tomatoes and cook for about 4-5 minutes.
7. With an immersion blender, blend the mixture until smooth.
8. Add the lamb, boiling water and salt and bring to a boil.
9. Cover the saucepan and transfer into the oven.
10. Bake for approximately 2½ hours.
11. Now, remove the saucepan from oven and place over medium heat.
12. Stir in spinach and garam masala and cook for about 3-5 minutes.
13. Stir in lemon juice, salt and black pepper and serve hot.

Ground Lamb with Peas

Servings|4   Time|1 hour 5 minutes
Nutritional Content (per serving):
Cal| 297   Fat| 12.2g   Protein| 35g   Carbs| 10.7g   Fiber| 2.9g

Ingredients:

- Olive oil (1 tablespoon)
- Fresh ginger (1 (¾-inch) piece, minced)
- Ground cumin (½ teaspoon)
- Lean ground lamb (1 pound)
- Water (1½ cups)
- Plain Greek yogurt (2 tablespoons, whipped)
- Salt and ground black pepper, as required
- Medium onion (1, chopped)
- Garlic cloves (4, minced)
- Ground coriander (½ teaspoon)
- Ground turmeric (½ teaspoon)
- Tomato (½ cup, chopped)
- Fresh green peas (1 cup, shelled)
- Fresh cilantro (¼ cup, chopped)

Directions:

1. In a Dutch oven, heat oil over medium-high heat and sauté the onion for about 3-4 minutes.
2. Add ginger, garlic, Ground spices and bay leaf and sauté for about 1 minute.
3. Stir in lamb and cook for about 5 minutes.
4. Stir in tomato and cook for about 10 minutes, stirring occasionally.
5. Stir in water and green peas and bring to a gentle simmer.
6. Adjust the heat to low and cook, covered for about 25-30 minutes.
7. Stir in yogurt, cilantro, salt and black pepper and cook for about 4-5 minutes.
8. Serve hot.

Pork with Veggies

Servings|5   Time|30 minutes
Nutritional Content (per serving):
Cal| 315   Fat| 19.4g   Protein| 27.4g   Carbs| 8.3g   Fiber| 2.6g

Ingredients:

- Pork loin (1 pound, cut into thin strips)
- Garlic (1 teaspoon, minced)
- Low-sodium soy sauce (2 tablespoons)
- Arrowroot starch (1 teaspoon)
- Broccoli florets (10 ounces)
- Large bell pepper (1, seeded and cut into strips)
- Olive oil (2 tablespoons, divided)
- Fresh ginger (1 teaspoon, minced)
- Fresh lemon juice (1 tablespoon)
- Carrot (1, peeled and sliced)
- Scallions (2, cut into 2-inch pieces)

Directions:

1. In a bowl, mix well pork strips, ½ tablespoon of olive oil, garlic, and ginger.
2. For sauce; add the soy sauce, lemon juice, sesame oil, Swerve, and arrowroot starch in a small bowl and mix well.
3. Heat the remaining olive oil in a large nonstick wok over high heat and sear the pork strips for about 3-4 minutes or until cooked through.
4. With a slotted spoon, transfer the pork into a bowl.
5. In the same wok, add the carrot and cook for about 2-3 minutes.
6. Add the broccoli, bell pepper, and scallion and cook, covered for about 1-2 minutes.
7. Stir the cooked pork and sauce, and stir fry and cook for about 3-5 minutes or until desired doneness, stirring occasionally.
8. Remove from the heat and serve.

Salmon with Green Beans

Servings|6   Time|35 minutes
Nutritional Content (per serving):
Cal| 235   Fat| 14.1g   Protein| 23.5g   Carbs| 5.6g   Fiber| 2.7g

Ingredients:

- ❖ **For Salmon:**
- ❖ Salmon fillets (6 (4-ounce), skin removed)
- ❖ Olive oil (2 tablespoons)
- ❖ Fresh parsley (3 tablespoons, minced)
- ❖ Ginger powder (¼ teaspoon)
- ❖ Salt and ground black pepper, as required

- ❖ **For Green Beans:**
- ❖ Fresh green beans (1 pound, trimmed)
- ❖ Extra-virgin olive oil (1 tablespoon)
- ❖ Fresh lemon juice (1 tablespoon)
- ❖ Salt and ground black pepper, as required

Directions:

1. Preheat your oven to 400 degrees F. Grease a large baking dish.
2. For salmon: in a bowl, place all ingredients and mix well.
3. Arrange the salmon fillets into prepared baking dish in a single layer.
4. Bake for approximately 15-20 minutes or until desired doneness of salmon.
5. Meanwhile, for green beans: in a saucepan of boiling water, arrange a steamer basket.
6. Place the green beans in steamer basket and steam covered for about 4-5 minutes.
7. Carefully transfer the beans into a bowl.
8. Add olive oil, lemon juice, salt and black pepper and toss to coat well.
9. Divide green beans onto serving plates.
10. Top each plate with 1 salmon fillet and serve.

Salmon with Lentils

Servings|4   Time|55 minutes
Nutritional Content (per serving):
Cal| 508   Fat| 21.9g   Protein| 28.2g   Carbs| 50.2g   Fiber| 16.2g

Ingredients:

- ❖ Green lentils (½ pound, rinsed)
- ❖ Onions (2 cups, chopped)
- ❖ Fresh parsley (1 teaspoon, chopped)
- ❖ Garlic (1 tablespoon, minced)
- ❖ Celery stalks (1½ cups, chopped)
- ❖ Chicken broth (1½ cups)
- ❖ 2 (8-ounce) skinless salmon fillets

- ❖ Olive oil (¼ cup, divided)
- ❖ Scallions (2 cups, chopped)
- ❖ Salt and ground black pepper, as required
- ❖ Carrots (1½ cups), peeled and chopped)
- ❖ Tomato (1, crushed finely)
- ❖ Balsamic vinegar (2 tablespoons)

Directions:

1. In a bowl, soak the lentils in boiling water for 15 minutes. Drain the lentils.
2. In a Dutch oven, heat the oil in over medium heat and cook the onions, scallions, parsley, salt and black pepper for about 10 minutes, stirring frequently.
3. Add the garlic and cook for about 2 more minutes.
4. Add the lentils, carrots, celery, crushed tomato and broth and bring to a boil.
5. Adjust the heat to low and simmer, covered for about 20-25 minutes.
6. Stir in the vinegar, salt and black pepper and remove from the heat.
7. Meanwhile, for salmon: preheat your oven to 450 degrees F.
8. Rub the salmon fillets with oil and then, season with salt and black pepper.
9. Heat an oven-proof wok over medium heat and cook the salmon fillets for about 2minutes, without stirring.
10. Flip the fillets and immediately transfer the saucepan into the oven.
11. Bake for approximately 5-7 minutes or until desired doneness of salmon.

12. Divide the lentil mixture onto serving plates and top each with 1 salmon fillet.

28 Days Meal Plan

Day 1:

Breakfast: Blueberry Oatmeal

Lunch:

Dinner: Chicken & Swiss Chard Stew

Day 2:

Breakfast: Spinach Smoothie Bowl

Lunch: Chicken & Berries Salad

Dinner: Stuffed Leg of Lamb

Day 3:

Breakfast: Chickpeas Toasts

Lunch: Tofu with Spinach

Dinner: Pork with Veggies

Day 4:

Breakfast: Oats Granola

Lunch: Prawns with Kale

Dinner: Beans & Sweet Potato Chili

Day 5:

Breakfast: Quinoa Bread

Lunch: Scallops with Broccoli

Dinner: Steak with Cashews

Day 6:

Breakfast: Spicy Tofu & Veggie Scramble

Lunch: Tofu with Kale & Chickpeas

Dinner: Chicken & Veggies Bake

Day 7:

Breakfast: Nuts & Seeds Porridge

Lunch: Shrimp & Veggie Salad

Dinner: Pork & Beans Stew

Day 8:

Breakfast: Oatmeal Cottage Cheese Saucepancakes

Lunch: Tuna Burgers

Dinner: Chicken, Rice & Beans Casserole

Day 9:

Breakfast: Tempeh Hash

Lunch: Chicken Pita Sandwiches

Dinner: Beef & Beans Chili

Day 10:

Breakfast: Tofu & Zucchini Muffins

Lunch: Quinoa & Veggie Salad

Dinner: Salmon with Green Beans

Day 11:

Breakfast: Lentil Goat Cheese Toasts

Lunch: Steak & Veggie Salad

Dinner: Black Beans & Pumpkin Stew

Day 12:

Breakfast: Dried Fruit Bread

Lunch: Tofu & Spinach Soup

Dinner: Ground Lamb with Peas

Day 13:

Breakfast: Veggie Saucepancakes

Lunch: Salmon & Beans Salad

Dinner: Beef & Pumpkin Stew

Day 14:

Breakfast: Tofu & Spinach Scramble

Lunch: Steak & Peach Salad

Dinner: Lentil & Sweet Potato Soup

Day 15:

Breakfast: Apple Bread

Lunch: Kale & Carrot Soup

Dinner: Beef & Raisins Curry

Day 16:

Breakfast: Spinach & Avocado Smoothie

Lunch: Chicken & Greens Salad

Dinner: Quinoa & Veggie Stew

Day 17:

Breakfast: Black Beans & Egg Scramble

Lunch: Beef & Mango Tortillas

Dinner: Meatballs & Spinach Soup

Day 18:

Breakfast: Broccoli Muffins

Lunch: Tuna Salad

Dinner: Chickpeas & Zucchini Chili

Day 19:

Breakfast: Oats & Quinoa Porridge

Lunch: Salmon Burgers

Dinner: Chicken & Green Beans Curry

Day 20

Breakfast: Tofu & Spinach Scramble

Lunch: Steak & Veggie Salad

Dinner: Lentil & Barley Stew

Day 21:

Breakfast: Nuts Granola

Lunch: Lentil Burgers

Dinner: Lamb with Spinach

Day 22:

Breakfast: Eggless Spinach Omelet

Lunch: Meatballs Kabobs

Dinner: Lentils & Quinoa Stew

Day 23:

Breakfast: Simple Oatmeal

Lunch: Shrimp with Green Beans

Dinner: Chicken & Kale Soup

Day 24:

Breakfast: Tofu & Zucchini Muffins

Lunch: Pork & Mango Salad

Dinner: Stuffed Chicken Breast

Day 25:

Breakfast: Nuts & Seeds Porridge

Lunch: Scallops & Strawberry Salad

Dinner: Steak with Cashews

Day 26:

Breakfast: Eggs with Spinach

Lunch: Chicken Stuffed Avocado

Dinner: Sweet Potato & Kale Stew

Day 27:

Breakfast: Green Tofu Smoothie

Lunch: Beef Burgers

Dinner: Salmon with Lentils

Day 28:

Breakfast: Greens Quiche

Lunch: Quinoa & Veggie Salad

Dinner: Turkey & Beans Chili